Fine-scale details in sacred places
evoke sensual responses while
reflecting community values,
cultural heritage, fine craftsmanship,
and shared experience capable of
nourishing generations to come.

John and Jody Roberts outside of The Cloisters in New York City
forty years after their first visit to the museum together. 2007.
Taya Roberts.

CHANGING
THE COMMONS

ORO Editions
Publishers of Architecture, Art, and Design
Gordon Goff: Publisher

www.oroeditions.com
info@oroeditions.com

Published by ORO Editions

Editor: David Moffat
Author: John N. Roberts
Book Design: Daniela Peña Corvillón and Camila Undurraga Puelma
Project Manager: Jake Anderson

Cover: Accessible elevated boardwalk and gathering areas, Muir Woods National Monument, California. 2016, Hanh Nguyen.

End Papers:
Front: Library Terrace Garden, San Francisco Botanical Garden at Strybing Arboretum
Edwin Hamilton, Stonemason & Sculptor. 2018, Jose Luis Aranda.
Rear: Restored lagoon at Muir Beach, Muir Beach, California. 2021, John Northmore Roberts & Associates.

10 9 8 7 6 5 4 3 2 1 First Edition

ISBN: 978-1-957183-33-6

Color Separations and Printing: ORO Group Inc.
Printed in China

ORO Editions makes a continuous effort to minimize the overall carbon footprint of its publications. As part of this goal, ORO, in association with Global ReLeaf, arranges to plant trees to replace those used in the manufacturing of the paper produced for its books. Global ReLeaf is an international campaign run by American Forests, one of the world's oldest nonprofit conservation organizations. Global ReLeaf is American Forests' education and action program that helps individuals, organizations, agencies, and corporations improve the local and global environment by planting and caring for trees.

CHANGING
THE COMMONS

STORIES ABOUT
PLACEMAKING

JOHN NORTHMORE ROBERTS

Dedicated to
Jody, David, and Taya

To my grandchildren: Maya, Seneca, Jack, and Ronan

 I have some stories I would like to tell you about places that I helped to create, both ordinary and extra-ordinary, and how they came to be what they are today. In reading them, I hope that you will learn something about placemaking, the work that I have done for many years, and in the process gain some insight into one small part of your family heritage. You may want to visit these places someday, and if you do, you'll have a perspective on why they are as they are and how this reflects the communities they were intended to serve. That may trigger questions about how other places, more familiar to you, have been made and empower you to think about how you can affect changes in your own environments. I would like that.

 First, some comments about placemaking. It's easy to think that a place has always been the way it is, especially the first time you see it if you have not been there before. But places are not static. They are always changing, both naturally over time and rapidly as environments are created. Rivers change course; mountains erode; sand dunes shift; birds build nests; worms cultivate soil; dogs dig holes; and people build buildings and roads and cities. Each subtle and dramatic action has a direct effect. One of life's great pleasures for me has been to puzzle through the hidden forces of change that have molded the places I encounter. I have learned to follow the water, and when I do, the stories flow.

 Your houses with their gardens were conceived and built as creative acts. And so were the streets where you live, the city where once was farmland, the farms where once was natural countryside, and the parks that preserve a bit of wild nature. Much of what we experience as part of our everyday lives has been affected by processes set in motion by someone long ago. It was a revelation to me to realize the extent to which our built environment has been designed. It was also revealing to understand that the world we have designed mostly reflects our narrow human frame of reference, not that of other living things, like salmon or trees. I came to see that it was well within my own power to choose to accept the conditions as they are, or to change them. And if changes were within my power, what voices would I listen to as my guide?

 Not everyone thinks about what it takes to make a place, or why some places are distinctive and others uncomfortable, or why some serve people and wildlife while others do not. People respond to places intuitively. They may not be conscious of why they react to a space the way that they do. I hope this collection of essays will raise your awareness of the places you visit. If, and when, you do think about such things, rich stories will emerge with insights about people, nature, how our surroundings have been altered, and the nature of the forces behind the changes.

 Placemaking is stimulating, rewarding, creative, and meaningful work to which I committed myself as a young man and continued to pursue for the following fifty years (and counting) as both a professional practitioner and college educator. I would hope that this work captures your imagination as it does mine but understand if it doesn't. At the very least, I hope the joy that I have found comes through in these stories, and that the stories prompt you to think about the places you inhabit in a different light than before.

Papa John

Left page: Elevated boardwalk at Muir Woods National Monument, Mill Valley, CA, 2021. JNRA.

FOREWORD

The writing of this book began as a love letter to my four grandchildren. Memories of shared experiences with them in parks and gardens, on trails, and in city landscapes fill my heart. Sense memories of places — smells, sounds, color, texture, space, wind — can be carried for a lifetime. I can see that such seeds have taken root with those youngsters. They have a joyous attraction to places where nature is celebrated. I was inspired to write to my grandchildren to provide context for this legacy. I wanted to introduce them to the idea of placemaking in our physical environments — to give them insight into the creative processes that have formed the spaces we inhabit. In so doing, I hoped to reveal the power within themselves to influence how places can be conceived. And not just physical places. If we imagine the enlightened transformation of our environment there is no limit to what we can achieve as individuals and communities.

While writing these stories, I realized that I was describing an approach to creative design that was in its infancy when I was in school fifty years ago and has only recently gained general recognition in the design literature. But community-based design from an ecological perspective has now taken hold and has become an important contributor to a new balance being created between the built and natural environments. It seemed that fellow professionals and ordinary citizens alike would benefit if stories like these, of the transformation of real places, were part of the public discourse. Placemaking is not a mystical, mysterious activity. It is the result of intentional acts by informed people. And with creative collaboration, magical things can happen.

And so I wrote these stories with family and friends in mind as well as fellow place-makers, students, and ordinary people who might find them interesting and useful as they transform their own environments.

The twenty-five stories included here describe changes to the physical environment in the public realm. These are not private enclaves, but spaces available to all as part of our public trust. I have organized the stories geographically by county in the San Francisco Bay Area and included a few from more remote Northern California locations. They represent my work over the past fifty-plus years in the form of neighborhood, regional, and national parks; community centers; greenways; downtown centers; neighborhoods; city streets; public gardens; wildlands; and publicly accessible commercial areas. Many projects include extensive ecological restoration. All have an ecological basis to their design. Some include historic and cultural resources. Others integrate public art. All are a product of community participation in the design process and reflect the values of the people who use and manage them. Many reflect a correction of past environmental or social assaults. And all aspire to redefine our culture's socio-ecologic relationship with the places in which we live. Taken together, they provide a window into the revolutionary environmental, social, and cultural forces that have affected our physical environment over the past fifty years.

The stories presented here also show how issues addressed in one location may inform how similar issues are addressed elsewhere. And the range of examples reveals that common ground can be found while creatively reconciling critical issues, even in the most unlikely of circumstances. Above all, the art of the possible requires building upon areas of agreement while weaving commonalities into a fabric that may hold diversity and inspiration and aspiration.

TABLE OF CONTENTS

PREFACE: PLACE, THE COMMONS, AND OUR SHARED LIFE IN NATURE

This book is about placemaking, and specifically places in the landscape commons. The places described are not "new," but instead represent adaptations of existing conditions to new sets of circumstances. All have been manipulated in some manner in the past, even those traditionally considered to be "wilderness" — a social construct that artificially separates humans from nature. But in each case a creative process of design has enabled a new identity of place to emerge based on inclusiveness, stewardship in lieu of ownership, and a layering of past and present, nature and the built environment.

These stories reflect the range of considerations that influence ecologically and community-based environmental design. Each place is individual and unique, providing responses tailored to the specific circumstances of its site. But the approach to design is common throughout all this work, and instructive. It begins with a set of broad questions that probe the central issues of placemaking in the commons. What do we mean by "place"? How do places sustain healthy connections among people and between humans and the natural world? Who is invited to participate in the place? And why focus on the commons? These questions are essential for anyone thinking about making alterations to the physical environment, because the effort to answer them provides key insights into the inherent nature of a place. The sense of place permeates our lives personally and communally, and its expression is the core aspiration of spatial design. Gaining a clear understanding of the nuanced identity of place is the essential first step in placemaking. It will inform all subsequent choices that are made.

"Place" generally refers to a location with a distinct identity. Places help us to orient in space and time. We organize our daily activities around them. They contain the stuff of our everyday lives and are part of the definition of who we are as individuals, communities, and cultures. We can feel safe within them or fearful because of them. A place can reflect a state of mind. You might say that you are in a "good place" or a "bad place" depending upon how you are feeling on any given day. Imagined places like heaven or the underworld provide a familiar grounded cultural frame of reference for explaining things that are not otherwise easily understood. An object caressed, the fragrance of the first rain, the sound of a train, the taste of a fresh peach, or the sight of a long-lost friend can transport a person instantaneously to a place deeply embedded within their sense-memories. Sitting on a bench enjoying a spectacular view is an experience of "place," as is cheering in unison with the crowd at the crack of a bat, wading in the surf at a sunny beach, or sharing a meal with a special friend. In each case, the idea of "place" carries a spatial connotation with physical, sensual, emotional, and cultural implications. It is essential that the multifaceted sense of place be recognized by the designer and inform whatever transformation is conceived.

For me, places are primarily defined by their natural setting. Humans and the places we create are a part of nature, not separate from it. The identity of our places is thus inextricably

Left page: Accessible pathways through the gardens at Green Gulch Farm/San Francisco Zen Center connect Cloud Hall with all other buildings. 2016. Hanh Nguyen.

linked to the ecology of a site. And the integration of nature with the built environment is a central consideration for placemaking in the commons. A protected bay, a fertile river valley, a waterfall on a granite face, or towering trees may give iconic identity to a specific place. But in each case, the underlying ecological systems and natural processes that sustain the life of a place are what create the conditions for such iconic features to reveal themselves, and are what interest me.

From long experience I have found that water is the key to unlocking the secrets of such underlying natural systems. Nature and the built environment are in a continuous dynamic balance with each other, adjusting as conditions change. Water is at the heart of it, and its treatment is the seminal consideration for the design of most of the places in this book. By following the water we can discover how to sustain the balance. Of course, in the end, nature will prevail. Entire civilizations have collapsed by neglecting the underlying ecological support systems for their built environments and it is often the water systems that fail. It is imperative for our survival and for the health of the planet that the places we construct nurture the long-term sustained ecological health of their settings, and water is the key.

Sacred spaces reveal the cultural heritage resulting from human use of a place. Places where special events have happened, places associated with important historic figures, or places where distinctive natural phenomena occur are often named in many cultures. The act of naming itself can provide insight into the cultural values of the inhabitants and the special relationship they have with the land. But spaces that are important to a community are not always named. Those places and their importance may only be revealed by probing, discussion, research, and observation. Societies and their special places change over time, but we can learn much by recognizing the sacred spaces of those who have lived in a place before us, understanding why and how they were made, and using that knowledge to respectfully inform new changes we make to build upon that heritage. Each of the stories of this book traces the influence of cultural heritage on the design of new places created in this manner.

The places described in this book are all in the public realm. They are thus places to be used and maintained by communities of people for common enjoyment. These are also places of inclusion where community bonds are nurtured, where community life is celebrated. And their composition has been derived from inclusive, participatory processes intended to give voice to anyone who wants to engage in the creative work of placemaking or enjoy the fruits of such collaborations. The participants and users of these places are their stewards, not their owners; they must therefore consider their value today and for future generations as a long-term part of the public trust, not as a resource for immediate gain. Meaningful, enduring placemaking depends upon the public and future generations having a voice in what places will become, allowing their voices to be found in the places created.

The stories in this book are about reshaping the physical environment of the commons — the shared spaces, resources, and natural systems that structure the daily lives of all living beings. Each focuses on a specific landscape that has been changed intentionally in response to its own set of circumstances as well as relationships with nature at large. No place exists in isolation; nor is an individual place the domain of a single entity. Natural systems like water, air, weather, fire, and wildlife corridors do not adhere to property boundaries. Actions in one place have a direct influence on the natural systems and human uses in others. Such interconnections can either nurture or contaminate depending on choices made along the way. As presented in many of these stories, corrections to past assaults in one place, no matter how small, can have a cascading positive effect. The more these interdependencies are acknowledged, the greater the benefit. It is the place-maker's job to discover the role that each place plays both in its immediate environment and as part of this interconnected whole.

The places in the landscape described here have been created for public benefit, conceived to enrich life among people and to nurture connections between humans and the natural world. As I look back over them, I can see a new set of cultural values emerging as we rediscover ancient wisdom about our relationship with the earth and the importance of community. These values are becoming increasingly apparent in our attention to the commons and to the design of public spaces. Such a shift in paradigm has been occurring both subtly and dramatically over the past half century, and our common future depends upon the extent to which we continue to recognize and nurture it.

BEGINNINGS

L et me begin by telling the story of how and why I started to do this work. I have always loved the out-of-doors, and spent much of my young life, no matter the weather, playing or exploring outside. My mother, Mary Jane (Jeri) Schultz Roberts, was an avid gardener and supporter of the arts with a keen interest in the beauty that a garden brought to her life. Her influence on me was immeasurable. As boys, my twin brother, Bill Roberts, and I also spent two summers in the central Canadian wilderness of the Quetico Superior National Park — an experience that was particularly important in forming my deep appreciation for places with vibrant natural ecological systems. While there were many other influences on me growing up, the visceral, tactile, and sensual lessons of my mother's gardens and living in that Canadian wildland of lakes and forests, canoes and portages, wild blueberries, loons and fish and beaver and deer have informed all of my work ever since. I also worked on construction crews throughout my teenage years building houses and gardens, developing practical tools of the construction craft, and learning to appreciate what it takes to build something, and build it well.

One incident in my young adulthood gave me clear insight into the potential healing power of a garden, with profound effect on all my work. Before Jody and I

Left page: Creekside patio and entry garden at Roberts's residence, Berkeley, CA, 2021. JNRA.

were married, we were both living in New York City pursuing our dreams of becoming professional dancers. Jody's young mother was near the end of a terrible struggle with cancer, and Jody was having a very difficult time dealing with the inevitable loss. One day was particularly hard for her. She was feeling sick, full of despair, and agitated. Our world in New York was mostly lived indoors — in dance studios, theaters, apartments — and on busy city streets having little to no contact with nature. Despite her objections, I got her to leave her apartment on that day and join me for a trip to The Cloisters at the far northern end of Manhattan Island overlooking the Hudson River. The Cloisters is a museum of medieval art built in the form of a monastery with gardens. Jody knew nothing about the place and rarely, if ever, considered gardens or nature as part of her world. Unsuspectingly, the moment she entered, she was stunned by the beauty of the garden spaces, the subtle composition of building and nature, the quiet contained views, and long vistas from the heights of the river landscape. A deep calm entered her body, visibly draining it of all tension. We stayed there for hours absorbing the space, the fragrances, the vistas, the birdsong, and the greenery. The power of that sensual experience transformed her, initiating a healing process from deep within and allowing her to return with joy to her city life, and to strengthen the bond with my life. I knew the importance of nature for myself and thought intuitively that it might help Jody. But I was not prepared for the profound effect I saw that garden have on her. It has lasted a lifetime.

By the time I reached college age, I was becoming aware that the natural environment that had been such an important part of my upbringing was under assault. I read in the newspapers that the Cuyahoga River, a large river that runs through Cleveland, Ohio, was so full of chemical pollutants from industrial dumping that the river itself caught on fire and burned for days. Water is the lifeblood of all living things, but nothing could survive in that river. And the Cuyahoga was not unique. The drinking water for millions of people throughout the world was then being contaminated by a toxic mix of pollutants, causing widespread disease, malformed babies, and death. Birds that normally would appear on their springtime migrations were also disappearing, poisoned by DDT, a pesticide that was sprayed on crops and in residential neighborhoods to kill plant-eating bugs, mosquitos, and other insects. For several years my father sprayed the foul substance routinely over our suburban Chicago yard, much to the dismay of neighbors. But the birds and other animals that ate the bugs were likewise dying, as were the animals that preyed on them. Fortunately, Rachel Carson's book Silent Spring exposed the horrors of DDT and spawned an international movement to ban the poison. It changed my father's views on the substance as well.

As a teenager, I didn't understand the science or engineering of what was going on, but I could see that nature was being stressed to the breaking point. Society in general was awakening to the extent of environmental degradation that had been wrought by our culture, and people were beginning to see how it threatened the underlying life-support

One incident in my young adulthood gave me clear insight into the potential healing power of a garden, with profound effect on all of my work.

systems of the planet. The movement for an ecologically based approach to living on this earth made sense to me. Awakened, I wanted to be part of it.

Worldwide environmental destruction was just one aspect of the complex human-caused turmoil of the times that would soon influence my life and views of the world more directly. Our country was then engaged in a senseless, ideologically driven military conflict in Southeast Asia, justified by officially sanctioned government lies. The Vietnam War, as we called it, was ravaging the countries in which it was being fought, causing the death of more than a million Vietnamese and hundreds of thousands more in neighboring Cambodia and Laos. The U.S. lost tens of thousands of people my age in the war, and my age made me a prime candidate for military service. The war was ripping apart families (including mine), destabilizing former trusted institutions, and causing riots and destruction in cities across this country. The unwanted prospect of being drafted into the U.S. Army forced me to abandon a budding interest in professional dance/theater. To avoid active service, I joined the Army Reserves instead. I then stumbled awkwardly through a series of jobs in what I came to regard as unfulfilling careers, including international banking, while beginning to raise a family.

Our lives had been profoundly disrupted by the war. But the disruption provided me an opportunity to explore different avenues in a search for meaningful work. And eventually I began to clarify my own values, set my own goals, and better understand the course I would like to chart in the world. I wanted to participate in the repair of the society that was being torn apart by war, injustice, and greed — to develop my skills and interests in the interest of meaningful transformation, not just the perpetuation of past ways of doing things.

What model could I use to focus my energies? My father, William E. Roberts, had been a corporate leader integral to rebuilding the U.S. economy following the Great Depression of the 1930s. Through his work he helped defeat the heinous Nazi regime in Germany in World War II, and he participated in the unprecedented U.S. economic resurgence in the postwar era of the 1950s and 60s. He had begun his career as a public-spirited executive for a Fortune 500 company that made cameras, projectors, lenses, and other filmmaking equipment used in the war effort and the film industry. He subsequently became the CEO of another Fortune 500 company that made video equipment and magnetic tape as

I wanted to participate in the repair of the society that was being torn apart by war, injustice, and greed - to develop my skills and interests for meaningful transformation, not just the perpetuation of past ways of doing things.

the high-tech Silicon Valley economy was just getting started. He and his colleagues were at the forefront of the postwar economic boom and technological revolution. For many years, his interest in the public good and his business successes reflected what was possible if we committed ourselves as a society to confront terrifying and complex issues head-on. But by the late 1960s times had changed, and he and other leaders like him were at a loss as to how to deal with the new realities. Once-beloved and enlightened institutions that had guided our country's emergence from the depths of the Depression and that had allowed us to triumph in World War II were failing, no longer trusted, and in many cases were themselves causing irreparable harm to communities throughout the country and the world.

As I was reaching adulthood violence was everywhere. The entrenched, caste-based racist heritage of the country was being broadly revealed to the public at large in the violent response to the Civil Rights movement — a violence punctuated by the assassination of inspirational leaders and simple activists alike. Police brutality, decrepit housing conditions, blatant discrimination, urban flight, the hated military draft, and decaying cities all combined to produce profound social unrest and demands for equitable and socially responsible ways of addressing the urgent needs of communities across the country. I wanted to be a part of this revolutionary change, but I needed to find my own way into it.

Creative, motivated people were needed to help rebuild the public commons, and in so doing, to help reestablish public trust and community bonds. This would have to be community work, not simply work for individual reward. Community building had a subtle and deep appeal to me. The commons is where meaningful connections with others are made, where shared experiences occur, where values are honed, and where creativity flourishes. I was discovering that I was more interested in helping to reestablish faith in public institutions and to restore the commons than in destroying institutions (which was an increasingly popular notion among my peers). I was beginning to see that I was part of a larger community, and that my skills, whatever they might be, could be used for public benefit.

I was raised in a segregated, affluent suburban world of white privilege. But in my twenties, I gravitated toward an urban world of creative arts that challenged most of the social norms I had known. During those years Jody and I thrived in the rich multicultural, multiethnic, and multiracial arts environments in which we immersed ourselves, first as members of New York City's Lower East Side theater world and subsequently in San Francisco, Oakland, and Berkeley. Our life in the city also brought us into daily contact with inequities and injustices exposed by the deep racial, ethnic, and economic divisions in the country. We experienced the energy, hope, beauty, and creativity that was exploding in the world of the arts in which we lived. We could see that our society's well-being hinged upon mutual interdependence, support, respect, and full acceptance among widely diverse communities. This was the world we wanted.

Correction of the problems we faced would have to include a component that would repair and reverse damages that our society had wrought to the places we inhabit.

A common thread among all the complex issues that confronted us at that time was that an equitable and environmentally responsible future was linked directly to the condition of the physical environment. Correction of the problems we faced would have to include concerted effort to repair and reverse the damage that our society had wrought to the places we inhabited. In conceiving better-designed places, we would establish a physical basis for changing lives and the course of our future. This would be challenging and meaningful work, and that appealed to me. With my interest in the arts, outdoor activities, and building things, I thought that helping to resolve problems of the physical environment was something into which I could sink my teeth.

With some research, I discovered that the newly emerging profession of landscape architecture was particularly well suited to address the multidisciplinary issues that needed attention, and my interest was piqued. The problems of the built environment were not narrowly architectural, engineering-based, biological, sociological, economic, or political; instead, they blended all these diverse concerns. A holistic approach to design was required within the context of the landscape commons. And the only profession that had begun training people to engage with the physical world in such a holistic way was landscape architecture. A wise, elder landscape architect, Thomas Church, who had designed two gardens for my parents, advised me to go to graduate school to provide myself with a sound understanding of this work, which had become far more complex than when he had begun to practice early in the twentieth century. He wrote me a letter of recommendation to attend UC Berkeley. When I was accepted, in 1971, Jody and I and our son David moved to Berkeley, where our daughter Taya was born.

At UC Berkeley I became an enthusiastic student of the profession under the guidance of an inspiring collection of teachers. They trained me to create places that are equitable and ecologically responsible; that nurture community and are sustainable over time; that serve multiple generations and cultures, are well-used, and respect diverse cultural heritage; and that are beautiful and give people joy. And after graduating I set out to apply my skills and creativity to make a difference as a professional landscape designer. After fifty years in the profession, I am satisfied that I have made a significant contribution to the physical environment. Considering the magnitude of the problems we have faced and the fundamental institutional changes that have occurred since my work began, my contributions have been small and incremental. But meaningful and influential change often happens in small steps. It may begin as small actions that affect people personally before being recognized as commonplace and then blossoming into a broader shift in society. Over these many years I believe that I truly have helped make the world a better place.

But there is so much more to do as we formulate visions for the future. Climate change, global warming, and sea-level rise cut across societies, demanding creative, enlightened, and equitable responses and new ways of operating. The ever-widening gap between the very rich and everyone else distorts how we inhabit and invest in our future. Reckoning with society's pernicious structural racism is also forcing us to face uncomfortable consequences of past choices. These new pressures will affect our physical environment. We must meet the challenge by sustaining an equitable socio-ecological framework for daily life. Generations before have risen to meet the daunting issues of their times with creativity, compassion, and joy. So will the next.

The stories, photos, and drawings in this book are about some of the places in the public realm that I have helped to create. All are located in Northern California, where I have done most of my work. All are creative adaptations of existing conditions to new circumstances, both large and small scale. Each creatively addresses pressing issues of our time, some more successfully than others. Each reveals the complex process of making a place, offering insight into the values of the place-makers. Not every project has been built, but each has hopefully contributed to public discussion about our common environment, the process of changing it, the people who make changes happen, and the people for whom they are made. ⊛

Right page: Stone wall made from 12th century Spanish monastery stones, Library Terrace Garden, Strybing Arboretum, San Francisco, CA, 2018. Jose Luis Aranda.

STORIES

to Humboldt County ← ● 23

● 13

● 14 ● 15

● 12

PLACES

● 8
● 7

2 1
4
3
5
6

● 11

18 16
19 17

● 10

● 9

to Yosemite →

21
22 20

San Francisco

SWORDS TO PLOWSHARES

FORT MASON AND THE FORT MASON COMMUNITY GARDEN
Golden Gate National Recreation Area Headquarters
Bay Street and Laguna Ave
San Francisco, CA

Right page: Walls of the community garden built from recycled concrete sidewalks contain an eclectic mix of plants. 2021. JNRA.

The work at Fort Mason and the GGNRA…taught me about the power of individuals and communities to orchestrate change to the physical environment.

I n the late 1960s, the federal government determined that many of the nation's military bases were no longer needed and that they should be sold off for development. The old military reservations in San Francisco and Marin Counties on the list included not only coastal open spaces important to adjacent communities but also irreplaceable historic cultural resources. Local activists were incensed that these places might be sold off so that private interests could profit by building housing developments or office parks. They and most of the rest of the public believed these lands should instead be converted to public parks or adapted for use by other public institutions.

Led by Amy Meyer and Dr. Edgar Wayburn of People for a Golden Gate National Recreation Area (PFGGNRA), local citizens mobilized and pulled off a monumental political coup. Capitalizing on the emerging environmental-protection movement of the early 1970s, they convinced the U.S. Congress to create the Golden Gate National Recreation Area (GGNRA) out of the former military lands in the two counties. As the first such federal preserve in an urban area, the GGNRA would create a new national park where people lived — not in a remote, largely inaccessible area. And, as imagined, this new 100,000-acre park would serve a broad spectrum of human needs while supporting the natural and cultural heritage of the place — a radical new and uncharted direction for the National Park Service. The former Fort Mason in San Francisco was to serve as its headquarters.

My first job after graduating from UC Berkeley's Masters of Landscape Architecture program was with Royston, Hanamoto, Beck, and Abey, a landscape architecture firm awarded the National Park Service contract to plan the San Francisco components of the GGNRA. My first assignment there was the GGNRA, a project that consumed my considerable energies for the following five years. Eventually, as I took on more responsibilities, I became the project manager for the transition of Fort Mason from a military installation to the national park headquarters.

Fort Mason had been intensively developed by the U.S. Army, and its conversion to a public park required selective removal of old structures to create an open-space network that would complement the remaining historic buildings and planned new uses while revealing the extraordinary landscape setting. Initially built in the mid-1850s for coastal defense on a strategic promontory overlooking the entry to San Francisco Bay, Fort Mason had later served as the primary point of embarkation for U.S. servicemen leaving for the Pacific Theater during World War II. As a consequence of that use, it had become cluttered with densely packed administrative buildings, barracks, a hospital, warehouses, roads, and ancillary structures. Clearing out the old, derelict structures while retaining the historically important ones — the warehouse buildings, the hospital, residences, and unique site features — would allow creation of a grand-scale open space worthy of the one-of-a-kind vista it offered of the ocean gateway to San Francisco Bay.

With sweeping views of the Golden Gate Bridge, Marin Headlands, San Francisco Bay, and other parts of the city of San Francisco, we believed Fort Mason's expansive car-free open space and historic building complexes provided a perfect setting for new recreational and cultural uses. Our plan was to integrate the palms that had once lined its roadways, its historic walls, and mature existing trees with newly created open space to create a gently sloping, sunny central meadow that would open to the west. Eventually, this Great Meadow, with its perimeter trails, hillocks, and links to the Golden Gate Promenade, would become one of the most popular informal gathering spots in the city as well as a premier venue for music festivals and other large outdoor events. But, first, the old concrete foundations, sidewalks, and slabs located there had to be buried on site. The displaced soil was then used to create earthen mounds and intimate spaces at the meadow's edge. Meanwhile, the lower port area, with its assemblage of historic warehouses, was converted into one of the city's most eclectic cultural destinations, providing space for more than 127 resident theater, arts-education, gallery, museum, cultural, environmental, restaurant, and activist organizations.

In the period after the closing of the military base many of the unused buildings at Fort Mason had fallen into serious disrepair. As those buildings had been removed, their foundation walls had been left in place. Some of the older apartment-dwellers in the adjacent Marina District, who would walk every day through Fort Mason to Aquatic Park to play bocce ball, had seen these derelict west-facing foundation walls as an unusual opportunity. In a kind of guerilla action, they had planted vegetables, fruits, and flowers in front of them to take advantage of the sun and reflected heat in a frequently fog-shrouded area of the city. When Fort Mason was being transformed into a park and the gardens they had been tending for years were lost, these neighbors spoke up to ask if there might be room in the evolving plans for new community gardens to replace them. This was not the kind of use the National Park Service was accustomed to, but it would be one of the first practical challenges it faced balancing the goals of the new urban park with traditional park policies. The park staff wanted to accommodate the gardeners; our challenge was to find a way to do so while respecting federal policies.

Archeological research revealed that the one remaining historic nineteenth-century barracks on the site had once had a vegetable garden associated with it, which the soldiers had used to grow their own food just below their parade ground. Plans called for this structure at the top of the hill to be stabilized and repurposed as an international hostel, and the old hospital below it was to be repurposed as the park headquarters. But nothing had been programmed for the space in between — the location of the former vegetable garden. This gave us the historical justification we needed to create a new community garden: it would be a modern adaptation of an important component of early life at the fort.

The new 2.5-acre Fort Mason Community Garden was built within a walled enclosure made of pieces of concrete recycled from old sidewalks, foundations, and slabs. The main area was flattened to improve access and terraced up the hill to take advantage of remnant foundation walls that reflected a considerable amount of sun and heat given the site's good southern exposure. The new walled garden area was also tucked behind a constructed earthen berm at the outer edge of the Great Meadow to protect it from westerly winds and screen it from the rest of the park. Garden plots were then laid out with areas for community gatherings, education, composting, and garden equipment/storage. An adjacent building was also later made available for cooking and classes. Thus configured, the Community Garden, run by its own independent organization, now has a five-year waiting list to obtain a plot. It is an exuberant, beautiful piece of community design that is considered one of the little-known treasures of San Francisco.

After Fort Mason's transformation was complete, Philip Burton, the dynamic politician who was the key figure in the creation of the GGNRA, died. His family wanted to memorialize him with a lifelike statue at Fort Mason, overlooking the vast park his legislative skills had helped establish. An invited competition was held to create and site the sculpture, and I submitted a design in collaboration with Wendy Ross, a sculptor from Washington, D.C., who knew Burton. Our concept was to place a larger-than-life statue of Burton at the edge of the Great Meadow, to the side of the main point of entry point, where he could be seen gesturing to the expansive vista. The statue would graciously invite people to look across the meadow to see the vast park that had been created. However, this was not what the family wanted. They loved the sculpture but wanted it, not the park, to be the main focus of the view. Politics and power were important to Burton — not parks, which were merely a political vehicle. He was an immodest man with a forceful presence. Another designer was selected to site the statue we had conceived, at the center of the view, providing a vivid lesson in political power.

The successful layering of uses at Fort Mason has charted new territory for the National Park Service. This is not a traditional national park, but it brings people into a place of reclaimed nature and provides access to the entire park system. My experience with Fort Mason and the GGNRA marked the beginning of a lifelong professional relationship with the National Park Service. My work has been rooted in understanding the creative ways in which public access and preservation of healthy nature can be interwoven for mutual benefit — a lesson I first learned at Fort Mason. The work at Fort Mason and the GGNRA also taught me about the power of individuals and communities to orchestrate change to the physical environment. This is another lesson that has become deeply embedded in all my work. ⊙

Following page: The Community Garden is at the site of the historic post gardens behind the Great Meadow and the NPS Headquarters building. 2021. JNRA.

PEACE PARK

CRISSY FIELD
Golden Gate National Recreation Area
Beach Street, Presidio of San Francisco
San Francisco, CA

Right page: People flock to the Crissy Field beach, bayfront promenade, dunes, and marsh at the edge of San Francisco Bay in all weather. 2021. JNRA.

The place had a power of its own, as well as an intact, although degraded, natural ecology. It was to be the underlying ecological systems that would establish the central organizing principles for the site, informed by complementary active recreational uses.

Doug Nadeau, the chief planner for the Golden Gate National Recreation Area (GGNRA), called unexpectedly one day with an unusual request. Dr. Ben Ichinose, the philanthropist founder of the People for Peace Foundation had been sponsoring the creation of peace parks throughout the world. Human connections with the landscape were central to these parks, which would nurture the idea of peace as a basic human condition, not merely as the absence of war. And he had requested permission from Doug to build one in the GGNRA. It was not unusual for people to approach Doug with suggestions for uses within the park, but at the time it was unusual for the proposals to include full funding. When Ichinose had called to inquire about possible sites, Doug had been looking out his Fort Mason office window at the narrow bayfront strip of the Presidio in the distance that badly needed attention. This remnant of the early military air installation known as Crissy Field was unlikely to receive government funding in the foreseeable future, but philanthropy might fill the need. He had suggested that Dr. Ichinose take a look at it.

When Doug called me, he was poring over the plans that Dr. Ichinose had delivered. The drawings proposed a Japanese garden designed by Katzuo Saito, a man recognized by the Emperor of Japan as a "Living National Treasure." Doug was apoplectic. Not only was there no precedent for a high-maintenance Japanese garden in the GGNRA or at the historically significant Presidio, but the Crissy Field area was one of the last remnants of an intact natural coastal ecological system in the city. A manicured Japanese garden was far from the kind of installation envisioned in the park's long-range development plans. Doug was calling to see if I might be able to help him find a way to balance these seemingly incompatible ideas.

Doug wanted me to collaborate on a respectful redesign with Mr. Saito that would reflect the planning and ecological context of the place while carrying the evolving plan through the byzantine National Park Service (NPS) approval process. He also wanted to maintain the relationship with the People for Peace Foundation. Dr. Ichinose agreed to my involvement. We further agreed my participation would represent the first-ever collaboration with a newly formed nonprofit support organization for the park. Thus, the Golden Gate National Parks Association would pay for my services, just as the People for Peace Foundation was paying for Mr. Saito's.

Crissy Field occupies much of the bayfront of the Presidio of San Francisco, which at that time was a fully functioning military base. However, the waterfront of the Presidio had been separated from the rest of the military base through an act of Congress. That act had intended to convert the entire Presidio to a national park, but as the legislation was being written, staunch objections to its conversion by Southern senators had forced an eleventh-hour compromise. A line was drawn down the length of Crissy Field, with the narrow waterfront portion of beach, dunes, and half the former airfield allocated to the GGNRA. The landward portion would also be within the national park boundary, but would remain in military hands until the entire base became excess to the Army's needs. The operating assumption at the time was that, since the Army would never abandon the entire Presidio, public access to a narrow waterfront band would be acceptable. The opposition Senators agreed because they believed a complete transfer of the base would never happen. They were wrong.

Because of that compromise, public access to the Crissy Field shoreline was circuitous at best. You had to know how to get there through the maze of military facilities. But people who braved the journey felt they had discovered a secret place that no one else knew about. To get the that stretch of shoreline, you first had to park your

Building place-memories while playing on a beach at the entrance to San Francisco Bay. 2011. JNRA.

car at the western end of San Francisco's Marina Green. From there, you had to walk along a narrow, jagged path squeezed precipitously between a steep rip-rap shoreline slope and an eight-foot-high rusted chain-link and barbed-wire security fence protecting the Army's motor pool (which had been inappropriately located along the shoreline). To make matters worse, the trail began at the city's sanitary sewer pumping station, making it seem further unlikely that it would lead to a prime recreation destination. It felt, instead, like you were sneaking into a place you weren't supposed to be. But once past the motor pool's security fence, the space opened dramatically to offer breathtaking views

The power of the landscape in
sustaining conditions for peace
– within oneself, with others, and
with nature – first learned at Crissy
Field, now infuses all of my work.
Each place can be a peace park.

across a windswept, little-used beach to the Golden Gate Bridge and Marin Headlands.
The sense of wild nature in the heart of the city was extraordinary.

The secret place turned out to have a small but steady stream of visitors at
different times throughout the day. But because they rarely encountered each other,
early morning walkers, later joggers, later dog-walkers, late morning/early afternoon
board sailors, native plant enthusiasts, and evening walkers and joggers had all come
to think they were the only ones who knew about this place and could claim it as their
own. Indeed, the revelation that there were so many different users came as a shock to
the participants at the first set of design workshops. Each would have their say, but they
would all discover that their beloved, secret place was not so secret. A key part of our
design for the Crissy Field shoreline would therefore involve balancing many different
interests while ensuring an appropriate level of environmental protection.

Mr. Saito's initial response to the place was to create an abstraction of a natural
landscape and to tame it as a garden. As a narrow strip of land with that offered limited
flexibility, he felt it important to "borrow" the distant landscape of the Marin Headlands
and treat the Crissy Field shoreline as a composed foreground that would bring the larger
landscape setting into the experience of the place. We agreed that the "borrowed landscape"
(the principle of *shakkei* in Japanese culture) was an important component of the Crissy
Field site, and that it should be used as a design strategy to reinforce the context of this
place within its larger setting. But as we discussed the inherent natural features of the site
and the characteristics of a place of peace in wild nature, a new design vision emerged.
The place had a power of its own as well as an intact natural beach/dune ecology and badly
degraded former wetlands. These underlying ecological systems could be used to establish
the central organizing principles of the place, informed by complementary recreational
uses. We would still "borrow" the distant landscapes, but for a public park in which people's

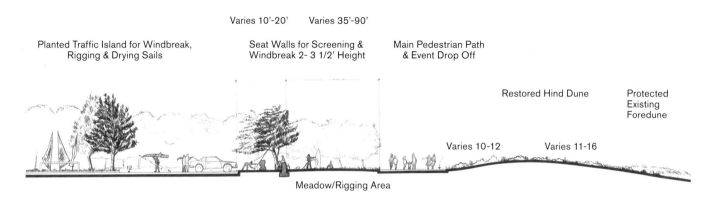

Conceptual design section of Crissy Field boardsailing area by the Roberts/Saito design team. 1986. JNRA.

Intense activity in harmony with the environment can bring a state of peace as profound as quiet, more contemplative activities.

active uses would harmonize with the natural life-support systems of the place. Mr. Saito had lived for 94 years in a remote coastal fishing village in rural Japan and had a deep appreciation for coastal processes, but ecological, community-based design of public spaces was not part of his professional practice. He therefore asked me to take the lead, trusting that together we would be able to integrate age-old garden design principles, recreation, and an ecological aesthetic to create a place of peace in a U.S. national park.

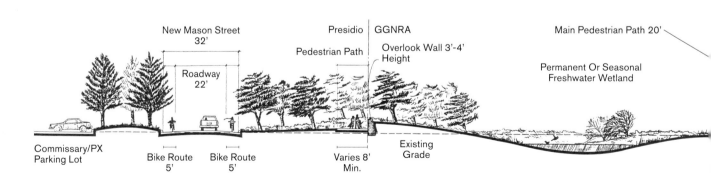

TYPICAL SECTION AT WETLAND

Conceptual design section of the beach, dunes, wetland, & promenade for the restoration of Crissy Field by the Roberts/Saito design team. 1986. JNRA.

As our work progressed, we discovered that the dunes and beach on the site maintained the same stable, dynamic relationship that had been mapped more than 120 years earlier. The winds howling through the Golden Gate passed over Crissy Field at an oblique angle, rather than head-on as typical of most coastal beaches. As a result, the sands that had been eroded from distant mountains and accumulated by tidal action had been blown along the coast to create an elongated pattern of dunes and beach. In a process sustained for eons, ocean and mountains were thus linked at this place. And, despite massive alterations to nearby areas by the military over the years, the beach and dunes had remained intact — a rarity for a waterfront in the heart of a city, and yet a symbol of nature's resilience. Protection of the beach/dune system was essential. Restoration of the wetlands behind the dunes would be more challenging.

In its undisturbed condition, the area behind the dunes had once supported a large fresh and brackish water lagoon and tidal marsh. The lagoon and marsh had been filled in over the years with debris and toxic materials — first by the Army beginning in the 1840s, then with debris from the 1906 San Francisco earthquake, and finally to construct the airfield. Yet, despite the destruction of the marsh, the underlying hydrological system remained: water still flowed from the uplands in the Presidio through pipes under Crissy Field into San Francisco Bay, and the tides still rose and fell in their diurnal rhythms. As we saw it, the reintegration of water was key to restoring the ecological health of the site. Water had also been a feature of Mr. Saito's original concepts. But the reintroduction of water would be severely constrained in our plans because the park controlled only a very narrow band of property.

Most of the original 130-acre marsh site remained within the military portion of the Presidio, and the army was staunchly opposed to its restoration. Instead of wetlands, the army saw the area as a prime spot for a regional-serving military shopping center with a large commissary, a post exchange, a post office, barracks, maintenance facilities, warehouses, and parking. Since the Presidio was within the national park boundary, the army's plans required approval by the NPS, and this was proving very difficult for them

SAN FRANCISCO BAY

Restored Hind Dune
Varies 14 -16

Hope Moore Picnic Area

Beach

Tide Level Varies
-1.9 to +7.2

+7.2

- -1.9

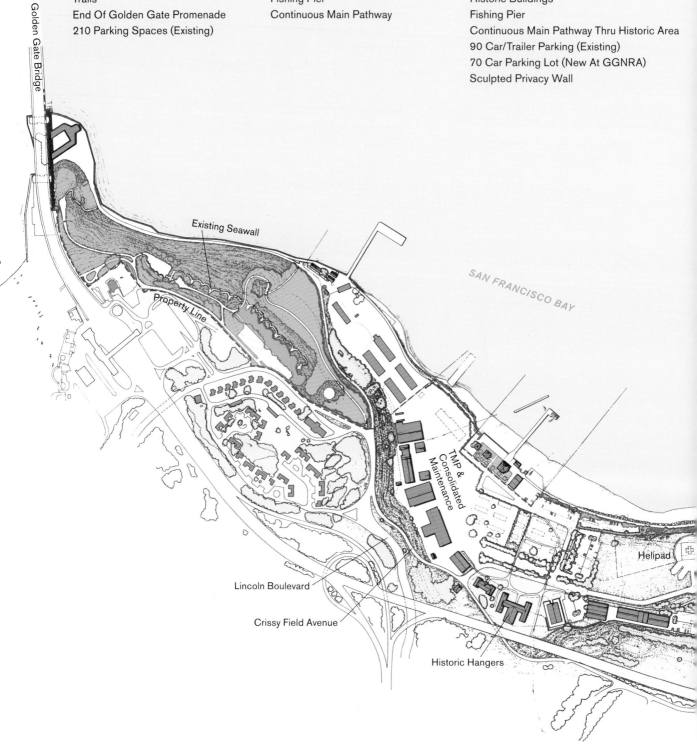

FORT POINT NATIONAL HISTORIC SITE (NHS)
HISTORIC AREA

Historic Fort And Fortifications
Seawall
Trails
End Of Golden Gate Promenade
210 Parking Spaces (Existing)

FORT POINT NHS ADDITION
HISTORIC & RECREATION AREA

Historic Buildings And National
Historic Site Headquarters
Fishing Pier
Continuous Main Pathway

WEST BEACH & COAST GUARD STATION
HISTORIC & RECREATION AREA

Continuous Beach
Small Boat Launch
Historic Buildings
Fishing Pier
Continuous Main Pathway Thru Historic Area
90 Car/Trailer Parking (Existing)
70 Car Parking Lot (New At GGNRA)
Sculpted Privacy Wall

Golden Gate Bridge

Existing Seawall

Property Line

SAN FRANCISCO BAY

TMP & Consolidated Maintenance

Helipad

Lincoln Boulevard

Crissy Field Avenue

Historic Hangers

Site plan for Crissy Field and Army Waterfront approved by NPS. 1986. JNRA.

100 200 300 400 500   1000 ft

CENTRAL BEACH
NATURAL AREA

Continuous Beach
Restored Dunes
Seasonal Wetlands
Fresh Water Pond/Wetland
Natural Grassland Meadows
Marsh Overlooks With Sculpted Walls
Continuous Pathway With Loop Trails
Native Trees For Screening
Controlled Access
Bike Routes Along New Mason Street
(Realigned)
Existing Cypress Grove Preserved
Boardwalks & Disabled Access To Beach
Site Art Acting With Natural Processes
Existing Foredunes Protected
Restored Hind Dunes
Self-Guided Interpretation

EAST BEACH
ACTIVE RECREATION AREA

Continuous Beach
Event Staging Area
Playfield
Multipurpose Building (3200 sf approx.)
With Public Restrooms
Lifesaving Tower
550 Car Parking Lot & 100 Overflow Spaces
Sculpted Parking Lot Screening Walls
Parking Islands Suitable For Rigging Sails
Existing Foredunes Protected
Restored Hind Dunes
New Dunes
Native Trees For Screening & Wind Protection
Bike Routes On Mason Street (Realigned)
Boardwalk & Disabled Access To Beach
Continuous Main Pathway (20 Feet Minimum)
Seawall (Transition Structure To Dunes/Beach)
Entry Grove Of Native Trees
Natural Grasslands
Informal/Flexible Meadow
Picnic Facilities
Entry Gateway & Plaza - Crissy Field & Presidio

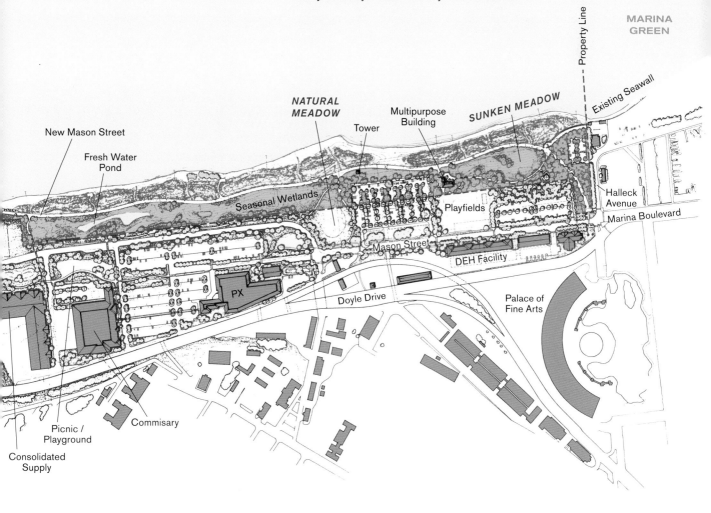

to obtain. We were hired by the army to integrate their waterfront plans with those we had been developing for Crissy Field. Eventually, a compromise was reached between the army and NPS management. The army would pay for the construction of parking and other recreational amenities within and adjacent to the park while keeping their buildings away from the beach. In return, the NPS would agree to approve the army's proposed developments on the site of the former marsh. It would thus not be until the entire Presidio was transferred to the National Park Service years later that restoration of the marsh became a real possibility and a potential defining feature of the area.

The site's strong and prevailing winds also had a direct bearing on the plans we developed. These winds are created by the displacement of hot air rising in the inland Central Valley by cool breezes that flow in from the ocean. The Golden Gate, the passageway carved by water between the Pacific Ocean and San Francisco Bay, serves to channel this wind (and the seasonal fog for which San Francisco is renowned), making it a keystone site in the ecological continuum of Northern California. The strong prevailing winds at Crissy Field just inside the Golden Gate, when combined with an outgoing tide, also create the conditions for a thrilling, one-of-a-kind, sail-boarding experience. And since a portion of the back beach area at Crissy Field lies in a wind shadow, the area offers both a sheltered location for sailboarders to set up their rigs and safely launch themselves and a vantage point for spectators to view the action. The site's unique combination of geography and regional ecology thus provides one of the world's best venues for this popular sport. Moreover, it serves as a powerful environmental education site, illustrating the relationship between climate, geography, and large-scale ecological processes.

In our thinking about the park, we therefore considered how intense activity in harmony with the environment can bring a state of peace as profound as more contemplative activities. And through a linear site arrangement that separated conflicting activities and combined complementary uses with shared facilities, our plans sought to balance the needs of the board-sailors with general beach and trail use and ecological restoration. In our final design we also proposed a broad, rustic promenade that would run the length of the beachfront area, unifying the experience of it. At a 20-foot minimum width, this promenade would be adequately sized to handle large numbers of people without crowding, while accommodating various means of travel. We felt one of the greatest joys this area could afford was simply being able to move through it at one's own pace, from end to end, alone or in a group, taking in the spectacular views, feeling the wind, discovering a bit of wild nature, and engaging with a variety of activities.

Although not present in its original form, the concept of a peace park still also underscored the Crissy Field shoreline we envisioned. The park would celebrate the area's natural forces — the coastal processes, the wind and climate, the spectrum of habitats. It would be a place of inclusion: competing uses would be organized to complement and support each other and allow people to enjoy their diversity. The park would also be expressly conceived as an integral part of a greater whole — a place to discover connections with larger systems and experience the environmental context through a "borrowed landscape" composition and activities that revealed the underlying forces. The simple act of naming it a "Peace Park" would also bring that aspiration to the forefront.

After six years of an intensive public design process juggling the needs of two federal agencies, the combined plan for the army's waterfront lands and the GGNRA's Crissy Field was approved to wide acclaim. Immediately after the NPS approval and amid the congratulating crowds, I was approached by Dr. Wayburn, the driving activist behind the creation of the GGNRA. He was delighted with the approval, the inclusive process, and our plans. But then he said, "We are asking too much of Crissy Field." I did not fully appreciate his comment at the time but remember thinking that he must know something that I didn't know.

Two weeks after approval of our plan for the Crissy Field waterfront, much to almost everyone's surprise, the federal government announced it would be closing the Presidio military base after all. I suspect that Dr. Wayburn, one of the most effective citizen activists in the country, was one of the very few people who saw this coming. And I also suspect he had a hand in it. I have since come to suspect that our plan and design process had become a catalyst for the transformation of the Presidio to a national park. What that process and the final, approved plans clearly revealed were the severe limitations of the artificial political boundary between the base and the park and the enormous potential of the entire area.

It had taken six years to develop a consensus plan for the shoreline in concert with the Army's plan for its adjacent lands. It would take another six years to transfer the Presidio to the National Park Service. By then, the GGNRA's nonprofit support organization had selected another landscape architecture firm to develop a plan for the entirety of Crissy Field within a larger park setting. That plan eventually built on our approved plan's consensus of user groups, mix and distribution of activities, broad promenade, ecological premise, and integration of water. It also included additional activities to broaden public use of the area at either end. With the entire former airfield now included in the plan area, there would now be room to re-create a tidal marsh on the former military land as the park's ecological centerpiece. But the new plan favored cultural uses instead, and the area allotted for the marsh, while more generous than in the originally approved plans, was too small to sustain a fully functional hydrologic opening to San Francisco Bay. Instead, annual excavation is needed to create a tidal connection to what is essentially a demonstration marsh rather than a self-sustaining one. A true urban/ecological balance is missing from this place, and a core principle of the original conception of the peace park was thus abandoned. Regardless, Crissy Field has now been transformed into one of the most beloved places in San Francisco and the managed marsh is thriving.

Jody and I were able to visit Mr. Saito in Japan before he died. He wanted to show me the places that inspired him when he was thinking about a peace park at Crissy Field. The venerable "Living Treasure" and the young American had bonded deeply, and he knew I would appreciate what he wanted to share. He assigned his son, a retired professor, to take us to Matsushima Bay in far northern Japan — which, with its magical, mysterious islands and dragon boats was one of the inspirations for the famous Ryoan-ji temple garden in Kyoto. We stayed at the home where he was born in the small rural fishing village of Katakai, and we were the first people of European descent his daughter-in-law and neighbors had ever met. He then escorted us to some of the beautiful gardens that he had designed and sent us to the great ancient temple gardens in Kyoto, Tokyo, and Kanazawa. Finally, Mr. Saito arranged for us to visit the Imperial Gardens as well as magnificent old private gardens like Murin An that were important to him. A rare personal and professional friendship with mutual respect had developed, which has had a deep influence on me. The power of the landscape in sustaining conditions for peace — within oneself, with others, and with nature — first learned at Crissy Field, now infuses all my work. Each place can be a peace park. ⊛

Right page: Kite surfing, board sailing, and other wind sports reveal the landscape-scale natural forces at play in this place. 2021. JNRA.

JUANA BRIONES'S PLACE OF HEALING

EL POLIN SPRING
8600 MacArthur Ave.
Presidio of San Francisco
San Francisco, CA

Right page: Benches on an elevated boardwalk overlook the restored ethno-botanically rich wet meadow watered by wetland seeps in the dunes. 2016. Hanh Nguyen.

The spring is the source of freshwater for the now-restored creek that flows north through the wet meadow to the saltwater marsh at Crissy Field Beach. Wild Nature has returned to the heart of urbanized San Francisco.

There is a place where birds magically reappear each year in far greater number and variety than any other place in San Francisco. They come to drink water from a spring known as El Polin bubbling from deep within the underlying serpentine rock, and from nearby seeps emerging from beneath ancient dunes that sit atop clay subsoils. Here the birds also feast on the insects, seeds, berries, and worms that thrive in a healthy, restored ecosystem. And the spring provides a major source of water for the restored creek that flows north through a wet meadow to the saltwater marsh behind the Crissy Field beach. This place was once almost unrecognizable, buried beneath the barracks, roads, and other facilities of the Presidio army base. But wild nature has now returned to the heart of urbanized San Francisco.

The restoration of this magical place is the result of a commitment by the Presidio Trust and its community of supporters to reestablish a balance between the built and natural environments at the former base. In other parts of the Presidio, as part of the development of an urban national park, historically significant developments have been preserved to sustain a community of residents, businesses, and institutional tenants. But in this area, at the core of the park, a complete natural ecosystem has been restored for all time, linked by an unbroken continuum of water-related habitats that extend from an upland valley to a new tidal marsh opening onto San Francisco Bay just inside the Golden Gate. To achieve this transformation, buildings were removed, the creek was daylighted, and a roadway that dammed up the water from the wetland seep was replaced by an elevated boardwalk, allowing its flow to once again nourish the meadow below it. A series of trail connections now complements these actions, allowing people to experience their effect. And exotic, invasive vegetation has been removed and replaced with species native to this site, which was once known in ethnobotanical circles as one of the richest and most biologically diverse in all San Francisco. Finally, to ensure a true ecological restoration, fill soils were removed to restore the contours of the site to those that existed before it was developed for use as a military base.

Through the course of its restoration, the area's rich cultural heritage, centered around El Polin Spring, was as important as its natural systems. Indeed, the two were intimately related, because this had long been a managed natural landscape. In the early 1800s, it was the site of the home and farm of Juana Briones, a woman of mixed Spanish and African descent who was a key figure in the early settlement of San Francisco. Raised in a small adobe house built there by her father after his retirement from the Mexican military, her life was deeply connected with this place. The house was also located near a settlement of native people for whom El Polin Spring provided a center of life. These were ordinary people sharing lives and cultures, and Juana was taught the healing arts by a native spiritual leader who made use of the rare collection of medicinal plants that favored and were nurtured at El Polin. Eventually, she, too, became a *curandera*, teaching herbal

A cascade of ponds in the daylighted and restored creek fed by the bedrock spring provide wildlife habitat in the heart of the city. 2016. JNRA.

medicine and midwifery to the next generation. Juana, her family, and neighbors also produced roof tiles, paving tiles, and adobe bricks for the construction of the Presidio from the dense clay soils that underlay the sand. And the abundance of fresh water allowed them to grow fruits and vegetables for the ever-expanding city.

Throughout the early years of San Francisco, Juana Briones raised a large family that included an adopted native girl, while also managing her burgeoning real estate holdings near the port. But as the city changed, so did Briones's life and the life of her children. Violently abused by her derelict, alcoholic husband, she convinced a local priest to annul her long marriage — an arrangement made possible only by having her husband declared dead. She then moved with her daughters and aunts to what we might think of today as a women's sanctuary home, which she built on Old Adobe Road down the peninsula in the town of Palo Alto.

Today the remains of the original Briones house, historic domestic site developments, and other archeological features are all woven into the design of El Polin Spring. Walking the site's trails or sitting on a bench on its elevated boardwalk, one can sense both the multilayered heritage of the place and the soothing presence of water and wildlife in the natural setting. The trail circles the enclosed valley bottom where water emerges, vegetation thrives, and critters make their homes, sharing space with human visitors. Here, in the middle of the city, there are no cars, just living things. The places to sit serve as outdoor classrooms for this, the richest and most popular environmental-education destination in the Presidio. It is a place to lose oneself to the sensual experience of a serene natural environment, along with some simple reminders of earlier inhabitants.

Although this place is today managed as a place of wild nature, the landscape of native brushy scrub and trees installed by the Presidio Trust's restoration team is likely different from the wetland seep and open meadow that would have been here when it was used by native people, or even by Briones. At that time, I imagine, this would not have been a place of untouched wild nature but one where nature was inhabited and managed to favor the growth of medicinal and culturally significant plants that served people's needs. By contrast, the landscape restored by the Presidio Trust is intended to represent unoccupied "wilderness." It is a subtle difference, of course, discernible in the feeling of spaciousness, the mix of plants, and the character of human interventions. It represents a reasonable course of action by the trust, which must think about issues of maintenance and limited funding. But I suspect that Indigenous groups would be interested in managing this landscape differently. At a deeper level, the present design likely reflects a cultural choice to emphasize nature rather than a balance between human habitation and nature. Yet, as a place occupied for many centuries, I believe the human/natural balance would have provided a more compelling story.

I find myself thinking about Juana Briones in this place and imagine how it might have helped form her into the remarkable woman she became. Places can have profound effects on people. She spent much of her childhood here, surrounded by plants that thrived in this location and by people who were deeply connected to this landscape. From them, she learned about the healing powers that came from that giving-place of nature, and she became a healer herself, before passing these lessons on to others. The place nurtured her, and she nurtured people in return. I understand from reading her history that this is the way she lived her life, and I like to think this was the gift of El Polin. When she finally needed to protect herself and her family from the terrible violence being inflicted on them, she was able to tap the inner resourcefulness of someone who had become aware of different cultural norms. I like to think that she learned not just the healing arts from the people of this place, but also lessons about justice and survival in her time of need — another gift of El Polin.

El Polin Spring is, once again, a place of healing. ✳

Following page: The accessible loop trail passes around restored native wetlands, meadows, and hillsides. 2016. Hanh Nguyen.

I like to think that Juana Briones
learned not just the healing arts from
the people of this place, but also lessons
about justice and survival in her time of
need — another gift of El Polin.

PAST AND PRESENT

PRESIDIO OFFICERS' CLUB
Presidio of San Francisco
50 Moraga Ave
San Francisco, CA

Right page: Gardens compatible with the historic building grace the entry and interior courtyards of the Presidio Officer's Club. 2014. Hanh Nguyen.

The building and courtyards were adapted to allow full accessibility – a unique challenge for an historic building constructed centuries before modern building codes. The historic integrity of the old building was intact, adapted for new uses, not simply a snapshot of a past moment in time.

The first European settlement in San Francisco was El Presidio, created in 1776 to overlook and defend the entry to the estuary that became known as San Francisco Bay. Located strategically on high ground, the first buildings at the Presidio (the Spanish word for a fortified military outpost) were made of adobe from the clay soils found just beneath the sand dunes there. The original adobe buildings were subsequently modified many times as the Presidio expanded. It was transferred from the Spanish to the Mexican to the American army, and the city of San Francisco grew around it. But a portion of that first building and its stone foundations still remain as integral parts of the structure that presently occupies the site. That building, in its prominent location at the top of a parade ground overlooking San Francisco Bay, still commands all that lies before it. Through the eighteenth and nineteenth centuries, adobe and wood additions gave it an impressive stature, and it became the Presidio Officers' Club — the center of social life at the military base. In the mid-to-late twentieth century, however, to capture views from a new bar and ballroom on the upper floor new additions in a modern architectural style were tacked onto its rear in such a way that they loomed awkwardly over the handsome old structure.

When the Presidio was folded into the Golden Gate National Recreation Area at the end of the twentieth century, the U.S. Army moved out. With no more officers in residence, the Officers' Club ceased to exist, and the Presidio Trust, which was overseeing the transformation of the base as a major component of a self-sustaining national park, needed to establish a new vision for the old building. We were hired as part of the larger Perkins + Will design team entrusted with restoring the historic building and its grounds while renovating it as a living museum, educational and cultural resource, and primary visitor destination in the park.

A top priority for the renovation was to detach the awkward, nonhistoric additions from the old structure so its handsome profile could be enjoyed from all sides. The 1970s-era addition to the rear was separated from the historic building by the width of a roadway that had once run through the site. This space was then transformed into a linear garden courtyard that could be used for special events, and that would bring light and air to those sides of the old and modern structures that opened onto it. The new courtyard is today contained at its northern end by a stunning Andy Goldsworthy sculpture, commissioned specifically for it, which is mounted on a tall wall screening the service yard. On its southern end it opens to an educational courtyard/archeology lab for the Presidio's archeology programs. Another awkward, nonhistoric addition at the north end of the building was also removed, allowing construction of a walled courtyard to serve as an outdoor extension of a new restaurant in the building's historic Arguello Room. Linked to the new interior garden courts, the Arguello courtyard has now become one of the most sought-after outdoor patios in San Francisco. It offers exceptional food and drink in a sunny location, protected from the winds, with stunning views of San Francisco Bay across the

A garden courtyard was created by separating the 1970's addition from the historic building. 2014. Hanh Nguyen.

Presidio's old parade ground. Thus designed, a series of new outdoor spaces have brought new life to the old complex.

Another important feature of the renovation has been that each portion of the building and all its new exterior spaces are now fully accessible — a difficult challenge for a historic complex begun centuries before modern building codes. One key to creating a seamless, unobtrusive new system for access involved the configuration of landscape spaces in concert with creative transitions at the building's entries. Most significantly, beginning with alterations to the street and sidewalk, the main entry has now been subtly altered so that it meets accessibility standards. These exterior spaces now rise almost imperceptibly to the level of a new court at the front door, cleverly incorporating the historic runnel that carries rainwater from the roof. With complementary plantings against the building, the slightly elevated sidewalk and roadway now also give an enhanced sense of importance to the main entry.

The federal guidelines for working with historically and culturally significant resources are very strict, and the Presidio Trust staff was vigilant in their efforts to meet the all-important Secretary of the Interior's Standards for the Treatment of Historic Properties. Among other things, this document specifies that the historic period of significance chosen for a facility is critical when it comes to defining criteria for its improvement. Since the period chosen for this old building was that of its earliest military occupation, we were given explicit and firm direction to re-create a bare earth and gravel ground plane around it, with minimal plantings. Since landscapes evolve over time, identifying a specific moment to preserve is more complicated than identifying the date a building was constructed. But the Presidio

Andy Goldsworthy sculpture on the wall in the garden courtyard. 2021. JNRA.

Officers' Club was one of the most significant historic structures in the country, it occupied a very prominent location, and its renovation was subject to intense scrutiny by the public and cultural historians. The staff wanted to follow the preservation rules to the letter, and this was the way they believed the building would have appeared during its most significant period.

The members of the Presidio Trust board of directors saw the matter differently, however, and they chose to challenge the historic "purity" of the NPS rules. In addition to its historic character, they were interested in the commercial viability and modern-day uses of the Presidio in general, and the Officers Club specifically. They felt that the development of the site around the building should be friendlier than the bare earth that would have represented its original condition. More than a museum piece, the place should be a lively, integral part of a modern Presidio, adapted to present-day needs. They wanted the landscape surrounding the building to create a lush, welcoming feeling, as a complement to its architecture, and they felt the historic rules could be stretched, particularly as these related to the gardens, which would have evolved over time in any case. The board eventually prevailed, and the result today are dramatic gardens with climatically appropriate plants integrated with contemporary sculpture. As a result, the historic integrity of the old building has been reestablished, adapted for new uses, and new gardens and courtyards create a complementary setting for daily use, not simply a snapshot of a past moment in time.

The Officers' Club is now one of the liveliest places in the Presidio. It provides layers of cultural heritage, gracious architecture, rich exhibits, diverse activities, and a commanding presence over one of the most dramatic settings in the Bay Area. ⊕

Following page: A new seamless accessible pathway flanked by gardens announce the main entrance to the historic building. 2014. Hanh Nguyen.

THE REVOLUTION'S EXTRAORDINARY ORDINARINESS

BOEDDEKER PARK
Eddy Street and Jones Street
San Francisco, CA

Right page: This Park in San Francisco's densest inner-city neighborhood safely serves children of all ages. 2018. Jose Luis Aranda.

A national model of ecologically sustainable and equitable site design. The actions taken in this park are small, incremental steps that most people won't notice when they visit the place. But taken together with other projects, they will change the world as we have known it for the better.

I n late 2009, we were invited to assist an environmental engineering firm founded by the son of one of my first students at UC Extension in the redesign of Boeddeker Park in San Francisco. Years before, the young man's mother, my former student, had thought I could provide useful advice for her son as he struggled to find a meaningful professional pathway. He eventually found his footing in ecologically sustainable civil engineering and art, and the firm he founded, Sherwood Design Engineers, is now a leader in its field. I was delighted with their success and enthusiastic to help them with what promised to be a most challenging and innovative project.

Boeddeker Park is at the heart of San Francisco's Tenderloin, the city's densest neighborhood. Of all the districts in the city, the Tenderloin also has the greatest number of families living below the poverty line, and it has one of the highest crime rates in the region. Fortunately, through the philanthropic largesse of a prominent San Francisco family, a previous lack of open space in the multigenerational neighborhood had been partially addressed years ago by the creation of Boeddeker Park. As an apprentice landscape architect early in my career, I had participated briefly and minimally in drafting details for the original park design with my first employer, Royston, Hanamoto, Beck, and Abey. That original design had featured a formal, modernist axial layout. From the corner of Eddy and Jones Streets, a grand, central pathway led through a number of handsomely detailed spaces, including smaller, garden-like recreational "rooms" on each side, to the park's anchor, its recreation building, at its far end.

Unfortunately, the well-intentioned original design failed miserably, resulting in an inhospitable, unsafe place that discouraged visitation. A subsequent redesign, which added fences for security, didn't improve matters much. Nearby residents reported that the park felt like a jail, and most were afraid to enter it. Drug dealers, gang members, and thugs established themselves at each of the narrow "pinch" points integral to the design, and were also able to control its entrances and exits. The situation eventually became so bad that its recreational amenities were removed.

It took the Trust for Public Land (TPL) to rise to the challenge and sponsor the redesign and reconstruction of the park. Through an extensive community-outreach process and close working relationships with the San Francisco Recreation and Parks Department and the City Arts Commission, TPL developed a radically new approach. The park was reconceived by TPL's staff as a spacious open area with fluid interconnections among various sub-spaces. Most importantly, a single access point would be established at a new Community Center building to allow monitoring and oversight of park users. Once inside, the park would then include spaces for people of all ages — infants, children, teenagers, and seniors alike — arranged around common gathering areas. All the park's features — outdoor fitness areas, community gardens, a full-size basketball court, a soccer lawn, climbing structures, toddler play equipment,

Following page: Multi-generational and multi-ethnic communities now co-mingle comfortably in the park. 2018. Jose Luis Aranda.

tai-chi plazas, and artwork — would be visible and accessible from the Community Center building.

The concept site plans developed by TPL were refined into site construction documents by a design team headed by Sherwood Design Engineers, for which we served as landscape architect of record. As a model of sustainable site design, the project also became a pilot project of the Sustainable Sites Initiative, a national program to integrate principles of sustainability into the basic fabric of site design. Globally, poor site planning and the use of construction technologies with high environmental impacts have been major causes of environmental degradation and rising carbon emissions. The project would provide a test case to help develop realistic requirements for urban park design in such areas of practice as sustainable materials sourcing, nonpolluting construction means and methods, strategies to minimize carbon footprints, water-efficient landscape design, ecologically based planting for habitat values, stormwater runoff and pollution controls, groundwater recharge, and recycling.

The central challenge of this project — beyond meeting the community's social, recreational, and aesthetic goals — was thus to normalize new ways of designing the built landscape that might help sustain the ecological and environmental health of local places and society at large. A paradigm shift will be required if our culture is to alter present, destructive environmental practices. In the design and construction world, this will mean fundamentally changing the ways we conceive and build things. It will also require the development of realistic, far-sighted, and enforceable standards. As a demonstration model, this project was intended to be at the forefront of that effort.

As evidence of the success in advancing a new standard of design practice, virtually all the rainwater that used to run off the site into storm drains and pollute San Francisco Bay is now captured in habitat-rich gardens, filtered, and recharged into the soil. Even the paved surfaces and play areas that can't drain to the gardens allow water to recharge through permeable paving. The reconstruction plans further

Safe and diverse park spaces encourage children to be children. 2018. Jose Luis Aranda.

mandated the salvage and reuse of most of the on-site materials slated for removal: this included concrete paving that was ground up and sorted for reuse, brick paving that was repurposed for wall veneer, reinforcing bars in the concrete repurposed as scrap metal, and sections of metal fence repurposed for use at other sites.

In terms of natural elements, all existing trees and undisturbed soils were preserved, and the total area devoted to plantings was expanded to occupy more than half the park area. The biological health of the soils was restored through the addition of herbicide- and pesticide-free organic compost and mulch. And revegetated areas used plants native to the region, supplied by nurseries certified in sustainable growing practices. These now provide critical habitat for native birds, insects, and other pollinators as a form of urban re-wilding that allows wildlife to reestablish itself in the park and in the surrounding neighborhood.

Meanwhile, all materials used for construction of benches, tables, play structures, walls, fences, and other features were certified to have high levels of recycled content to capture the embedded carbon. These were largely supplied from within the region to limit the transportation impacts, and the structures themselves were designed for easy disassembly and salvage for reuse in the future. Finally, requirements for ongoing pollution controls, emission controls, storage and recycling, sustainable site maintenance, and energy use by the construction contractors were included in the project construction manual.

The park reopened in 2014, and immediately became one of the most beloved and heavily used neighborhood parks in San Francisco. It now offers a welcoming, lively, and safe place full of people throughout the day, and it serves as a center for evening activities as well. In this distressed neighborhood it provides a place of beauty, full of joy, serving as a hub of community activity and a haven for thousands of children. It is a pleasure to visit there today and see a diverse mix of family groups playing and socializing in a rich, stimulating, and supportive environment. And because of its certification through the Sustainable Sites Initiative, it has also become a national model of ecologically sustainable and equitable site design. Yet part of the magic of the place is that its sustainable features are so seamlessly integrated into its fabric that their ordinariness is extraordinary. They support community gatherings and recreational activities while at the same time radically changing the way in which the built environment relates to a larger environmental setting.

Because of the success of beautifully crafted projects like this, with demonstrated environmental benefits and cost efficiencies, most of the features of this and other pilot projects have become standard procedures in both the building industry and the regulatory framework throughout the country. The actions taken in this park were small incremental steps that most people won't notice when they visit. But taken together with other projects, they will change the world as we have known it for the better. ⊙

Following page: The Community Center building by WRNS STUDIO, Architects anchors the park's activities. 2016. Hanh Nguyen.

THE STONEMASON'S SIGNATURE

LIBRARY TERRACE GARDEN
San Francisco Botanical Garden at Strybing Arboretum
Golden Gate Park at the 9th Street Entrance
San Francisco, CA

Right page: A wall made of repurposed salvaged stones from a 12th century Spanish monastery encloses the garden. 2018. Jose Luis Aranda.

In all the years of its existence, the Arboretum had never had such a place for visitors to simply gather and sit.

T he publishing tycoon William Randolph Hearst once dreamed of rebuilding a twelfth-century Spanish monastery complex in Northern California. But after he had purchased and disassembled all its various structures, his accountants convinced him he could no longer afford to do so. Like many others, he had lost a fortune in the Great Depression, and so he abandoned the project. The buildings' carved stones, however, numbered for ease of reconstruction by his architect, Julia Morgan, had already been packed onto three ships then sailing to the West Coast. And, upon arrival, they were removed from the docks and unceremoniously dumped in a remote section of Strybing Arboretum in San Francisco's Golden Gate Park.

Over the years some of the stones appeared in the gardens of wealthy Arboretum patrons. Others were placed in strategic locations within the park, and others were used as edging for pathways in the arboretum itself. At one point, a group of Cistercian monks from Chico, CA, was granted permission to remove all the stones for one of the original monastery buildings, to rebuild it on their property. But mostly, the stones just sat there throughout the twentieth century. Eventually, as word got out that the stones were available, several gardens within the arboretum (also known today as the San Francisco Botanical Garden), were constructed with them, most notably the California Native Plant Garden.

I was invited to design a garden for the botanical garden's Helen Crocker Russell Library. Its siting meant it would be the first garden that visitors would encounter upon entering the arboretum, with a direct connection from the main pathway just beyond the entry gates. The space would also serve as an outdoor terrace for the library, with access from inside through a new doorway that replaced a window. Plans called for the garden to accommodate special events, provide a location for docents to meet their tour groups, and offer a place for visitors to simply sit in the sun in the cool foggy climate while overlooking the arboretum. In all the years of its existence, the Strybing Arboretum had never had such a place.

The main arboretum path next to the garden was already lined with stone blocks from the medieval monastery. One of the primary charges given to me by the director of the arboretum was to use them and to integrate additional remnant stones from the pile remaining within the park. When I went to look at the remnant stones, I discovered that simple, rectangular blocks like those seen throughout in the botanic garden were mostly gone. Instead, the stones available for the new garden were far more elaborately shaped. Among them were intricately carved fluted column bases, curved ribbing for vaulted arches, keystones for the tops of arches, and a variety of other irregular and astonishing shapes created by master medieval stonemasons. I was stunned by the beauty of the individual pieces and excited about the potential for incorporating them into the new garden composition.

The garden would be a welcoming, mostly paved space interwoven with plantings from the arboretum's Asian Plant Collection. Its main gathering area, flowing directly from the library, would overlook the arboretum, with smaller more intimate spaces and benches to the sides. A small fountain in the main gathering area, donated in remembrance of a longtime patron, would create a visual link to the large fountain in the distance at the center of the botanic garden. And the entire space would be contained by a three-foot-high stone wall with integrated seating, all to be built with the irregular medieval carved stones. Offering both prospect and refuge, this would be a gracious, intimate, and richly textured space.

I had an idea of how the stones could be assembled to create the perimeter wall and did a series of sketch elevations to convey my intent, which were enthusiastically approved by the arboretum director and staff. But the big question for me was, who would be able to build such a feature? I knew of no stonemasons who might take on this work. The answer came quite unexpectedly as we wrestled with the fountain.

The donors of the fountain asked that the arboretum director and I find a suitable one for them. We located a beautiful and simple stone fountain at a new outdoor sculpture gallery under the BART tracks in nearby Berkeley, and the donors approved its purchase. I then had the idea that the sculptor of the fountain might be interested in talking with me about building the wall, and the director agreed that should I speak with him. We discovered that the sculptor, Edwin Hamilton, was a stonemason by trade and did stone sculpture in his spare time. He jumped at the opportunity to build the wall, thus marking the beginning of a very long and fruitful association between Edwin and me.

Edwin looked at the pile of abandoned stones and sent me a sketch proposal of an idea he had. The drawing was difficult to decipher. Neither the director nor I could understand what was being proposed. The director said that she thought we had made

Artifacts created centuries ago in a different culture and faraway place - plundered, discarded and abandoned - have been artfully reassembled with dignity to structure this modern space. Old and new are bound together to create a place of community.

This would be a gracious, intimate, and richly textured space with a protected overview of the larger Arboretum – prospect and refuge.

a mistake, and that we should probably look for someone else to do the work. I advised patience. Not everyone thinks and communicates alike; I wanted to meet with Edwin at the stone pile to see if he could show me what he was thinking. I understood that he made things out of stone — he didn't draw. After we gathered several of the curved ribbing pieces that had been part of a vaulted arch, Edwin and I leaned the heavy pieces together at his direction, balancing them delicately in an alternating pattern that began to resemble a kind of abstract lattice of carved objects. The effect was breathtaking to me. While celebrating the beauty of the old stonework, by simply turning the pieces around and establishing new relationships among them he had created something entirely new. He clearly saw a way to use the old stones that would honor and reveal their nature as twelfth-century stonemasonry while masterfully assembling them into a distinctive, open, lattice-like textured wall for the entrance to this new garden. I suggested that we leave the model we had just created in place at the stone pile and have the director and her board come by to see it. Once they saw what was being proposed, they understood and instructed us to proceed immediately with the wall.

As Edwin dove into the construction and began assembling pieces in ways that combined his insights with my original intent, he carefully cut some of the old, plain stones to fit seamlessly with the more intricately carved stones. He and I were both aware that we were altering the creative work of centuries-old artisans to build something new. But we approached the work with a deep respect for what had been done before and an eye to revealing the essence of the individual pieces. Besides, in our disposable modern culture the stones had become detritus, and we were finding a way to reuse them that would again highlight their beauty. Through a new act of craftsmanship, we would link centuries together.

Edwin discovered that several of the more complex stones had markings incised into them that became visible when the sun cast shadows at a low angle. Some of the markings appeared to be twelfth-century construction lines. Thus, a center point with neatly incised rays described where the fluting for a column would go, and other incisions revealed how a calculated geometry was used to carve even the most elaborate

Following page: Fluted column bases and other ancient carved stones form a bench at the Arboretum's Library Terrace. 2018. Jose Luis Aranda.

Page 86: The garden terrace is a place to gather and overlook the Arboretum. 2018. Jose Luis Aranda.

pieces. Indeed, they revealed the very structure of the medieval stonemason's art. Edwin then pointed out other marks that he had found — large and small Xs and other symbols in varying patterns. He believed these represented the signatures of various different stonemasons. The signatures reflected a certain pride of accomplishment, an acknowledgement of authorship. But they might also have served as a way of tallying production, because each mason was likely paid only on the basis of each stone carved. These discoveries led us to decide to construct the seating portion of the wall with these incised patterns open to view so that the human side of the stonemasons' art would be revealed to people as they sat in the garden.

The wall enclosing the garden is today as much a work of sculpture itself as it is a tour-de-force in stonemasonry. It is a stone assembly unlike any other. Remnant pieces of a twelfth-century monastery have been transformed into a new garden wall in a way that celebrates two moments of creativity linked across centuries. Stones carved in a faraway

place by a different culture — plundered, discarded, and abandoned in San Francisco by a more recent culture — have been artfully reassembled with dignity to structure this modern space featuring plants from yet another continent. Old and new are bound together to create a place of community. An integral part of a new place and time, the beautiful multilayered public garden builds upon a rich and varied cultural heritage to create a touchstone for future generations.

People who visit the Helen Crocker Russell Library Terrace Garden will experience a place of subtle textures, natural beauty, and respite overlooking the lush and spacious arboretum. They may not see the intimate humanity of the stonemason's art or appreciate the respectful blending of the ancient and modern, or even recognize the level of cultural diversity embedded in this garden as a place. The spatial aesthetic of a landscape is a sensual one. Nevertheless, visitors will sense a settled calm here that accompanies a place of nature linked with ancient stones, and they will know they are in a special place. ◉

COHO RE-WILDING
Lower Redwood Creek Restoration and Public Access, Muir Beach

INTERWOVEN IN THE FOREST FLOOR
Muir Woods National Monument

Marin County

COHO RE-WILDING

LOWER REDWOOD CREEK RESTORATION AND PUBLIC ACCESS
Golden Gate National Recreation Area
Pacific Way at CA State Highway 1
Muir Beach, CA

Right page: The pedestrian bridge across the floodplain and creek brings visitors directly into contact with wild nature while protecting the habitat. 2016. Hanh Nguyen.

By mistaking rural scenery for wild nature, clues to the underlying disturbances went unseen by most visitors for decades. Coho Salmon proved to the be the key indicator. The cultural disconnection with healthy wild nature has had devastating consequences for the entire watershed.

The hopeful story of the 35-acre wetland restoration and public access improvements at Muir Beach features good intentions gone awry, cultural biases, high-stakes political maneuvering, enlightened site design, the precarious existence of endangered species, and critical lessons in ecological design. The very conception of the project, within a frame of reference that emphasizes the health of a watershed, also reflects a shift in cultural values, as our society learns to live with nature rather than attempting to dominate it.

For thousands of years people have lived in and flourished in the Redwood Creek watershed and at Muir Beach, where the creek meets the ocean. Since Europeans first settled in California, and particularly since the late nineteenth century, this area of Marin County has provided one of the most popular recreation destinations in the San Francisco Bay Region, and one of the closest to the major population centers of the East and North Bay counties. Muir Beach, the beach and its associated community, today occupy a scenic rural setting where the creek joins the ocean after passing through one of the world's most biologically rich small watersheds. The wetlands along Redwood Creek at Muir Beach are the ecological centerpiece of the watershed. Whatever happens at Muir Beach affects the entire watershed, and whatever happens within the watershed affects Muir Beach.

The Muir Beach area has been altered over the past 150 years in subtle and dramatic ways, all in plain sight, with devastating consequences. Most visitors today may also be unaware of the severity of the human-caused environmental damage that has taken place upstream in the Redwood Creek watershed, which today includes Mt. Tamalpais State Park and Muir Woods National Monument. People who are unfamiliar with healthy wildland ecology may perceive Muir Beach and its surrounding landscape as a pleasant rural open space with trees, streams, fresh air, agriculture, and an ocean beach. By mistaking rural scenery for wild nature, however, clues to the underlying disturbances went unseen for decades. The health of the coho salmon in Redwood Creek told another story, however. The creek once hosted a legendary number of the fish, which hatch from eggs deposited there and then spend three years at sea before returning to spawn. Yet watershed-wide destruction of the salmon habitat decimated the wild coho population, placing it in imminent danger of total collapse. And the cultural disconnection with healthy wild nature made evident by the decline of this key indicator species had further devastating consequences for the entire watershed.

Assaults on the environment can be found throughout the area of Redwood Creek. The beach, dunes, backwater wetlands, and upland forests have each been systematically exploited for human use and resource extraction. Extensive logging of old-growth redwood and Douglas fir, combined with uncontrolled cattle grazing and unsustainable creek alterations, fundamentally destabilized both the hydrologic system and the soils. And soil erosion as a result of logging, grazing, and creek alterations has

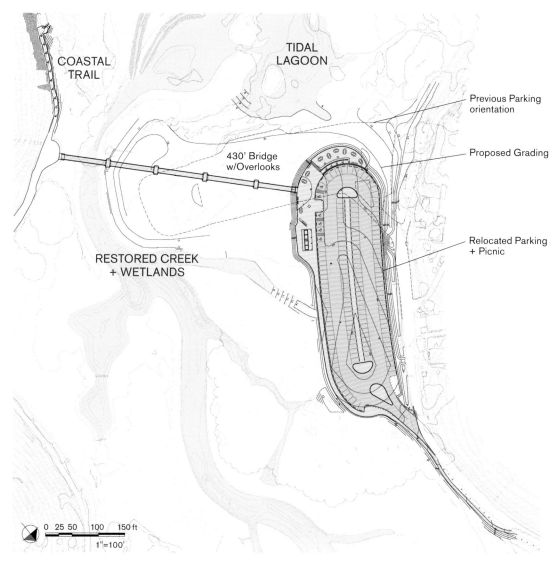

COASTAL TRAIL

TIDAL LAGOON

Previous Parking orientation

Proposed Grading

430' Bridge w/Overlooks

Relocated Parking + Picnic

RESTORED CREEK + WETLANDS

0 25 50   100   150 ft

1"=100'

Diagram showing proposed relocated parking, restored creek and wetlands, and pedestrian bridge. 2011. JNRA.

continued to this day, spreading upstream into all the side canyons. One result was that by the mid-twentieth century, the once biologically rich freshwater lagoon and marsh behind the beach dunes, known as Big Lagoon, had mostly been filled in with soil eroded from disturbed uplands. The dunes, too, were mined for sand, and a funky resort hotel, popular with counter-culture rock bands of the 1960s, was constructed right on the beach. The final blow to Big Lagoon came when the creek was physically moved out of the valley floor to a new, "more convenient" location behind constructed levees, and the remaining marsh was filled in to create a horse pasture.

Aerial of Muir Beach, post construction, with restored creek, floodplain, dunes, and wetlands; relocated parking; and trail connection across the 430' pedestrian bridge. 2014. JNRA.

By the early 1970s help was on the way. The beach and most of the watershed became part of an extensive new public park and open-space preserve, setting the stage for ecological restoration throughout the watershed. The restoration of Redwood Creek at Muir Beach would be one of the highest priorities for the newly formed Golden Gate National Recreation Area (GGNRA). But years passed before any actions were taken, as federal funding for restoration could not be found. Finally, in the mid-1980s, an unexpected breakthrough came from the unlikeliest of sources. Severe winter storms had washed away a portion of California's coastal Highway 1 at an oceanside cliff north of Muir Beach.

The essence of ecological design is the
establishment of sustainable resilient
natural processes that will support the
natural wonders. It is not the design
of the wonders themselves. It is a way
of living with nature, rather than
imposing one's will on nature.

To rebuild it, Caltrans, the California State highway agency, received permission from
the newly established State Coastal Commission to push debris from the landslide into
the ocean's intertidal zone. But this would only be allowed if Caltrans would fund the
restoration of the degraded wetlands at Muir Beach. By a twist of fate, as mitigation for
the destruction of the tidal marsh at the washout, Caltrans would pay for restoration of
wetlands and improved public access at Muir Beach!

I was hired by Caltrans as a member of a multidisciplinary design team headed by
Philip Williams Associates, a renowned and pioneering ecological engineering hydrology
firm that would lead the project. Working collaboratively with the engineers and National
Park Service staff, we developed a number of different approaches to the restoration of the
35-acre site's wetlands and creek in combination with a new layout for its parking lots, trails,
restrooms, and recreational facilities. The alternative plans were reviewed extensively with
the local community, technical experts, regulatory agencies, national and state park staff,
and other interested stakeholders. And by the end of a multiyear design and environmental
review process, the consensus of the participants was that Caltrans should proceed with
plans to re-create the original, historic Big Lagoon that had been destroyed over the
preceding 150 years. The common belief was that this would be the key to reestablishing
a healthy natural system that would allow the return of the coho salmon. Broad support
for this plan was found throughout the community of highly educated and passionate
proponents of restored ecological systems. However, we were not aware at the time of the
cultural biases that lay behind this consensus.

As the preferred plan was proceeding through the final approval and environmental
review process in the mid-1980s, it suffered a major setback. Caltrans decided that the

project was simply too expensive and open-ended, and decided they wanted to get out of the deal they made to pay for it. They learned that a prime piece of property in western Marin County at the southern end of Tomales Bay near Point Reyes National Seashore, that the National Park Service had wanted for years, was coming up for sale. The heirs of the Giacomini Ranch were interested in selling this land, but the National Park Service could not act fast enough to buy it. Instead, Caltrans leapt at the opportunity, offering to buy the property and donate it to the national park in exchange for being let off the hook for the Muir Beach restoration. The executives at the GGNRA accepted the Caltrans offer and, in so doing, halted work at Muir Beach for the next ten years. Ultimately, this was a delay that would benefit the project by allowing time for research and reconsideration of priorities. By the mid-1990s, federal funding had finally become available, and with a new federal commitment the project resumed, with additional assistance from the recently formed nonprofit Golden Gate National Park Conservancy.

During the ten-year hiatus, scientists at the GGNRA had been actively researching soil erosion in the Redwood Creek watershed, in part inspired by the preferred plan to restore Big Lagoon. What the scientists discovered fundamentally changed the course of the project. They found that the process of erosion that had begun with widespread deforestation and uncontrolled cattle grazing was continuing virtually unabated, despite valiant efforts within the watershed to change such destructive land-management practices. While the downstream areas had finally been stabilized at a new lower elevation, the stream hydrology had been thrown out of balance. The scientists projected that steady, continuous erosion would continue for decades throughout the upper watershed, with high volumes of sediments washing down until a new balance could be established.

The implication of this discovery for restoring Big Lagoon was profound. The consensus plan to restore it would already require a massive effort to remove the dirt that had

The visitor has come seamlessly into contact with wild nature by design - an experience that will become embedded into the memories of this place and a point of reference for future encounters with nature.

Picnic area/outdoor classroom at marsh overlook, 2019. JNRA.

accumulated over the years at the site it had previously occupied. But what the scientists had just pointed out was that the soil that was continuing to be eroded from the upper watershed and carried by the creek toward the ocean would quickly fill in the hole created for a new lagoon. A newly excavated Big Lagoon would thus be mostly gone within just a few decades. The historic Big Lagoon, in its natural state, had been a byproduct of an ever-changing geomorphology that had evolved over time. As a shifting landscape feature, it had been sustained by a dynamic balance among the forces of erosion, natural water flow, forest cover and stabilizing roots, and varying levels of ocean tides and storm swells. In other words, Big Lagoon was not just a fixed object like a building that could be re-created. In its original state

it had been a physical expression of a dynamic system, and that system had been changed so dramatically by human interventions over the past century that it was unlikely that a reestablished lagoon could be sustained naturally under the current conditions.

We and our elite collaborators had made a fundamental, rookie error in ecological design. We had focused on an ephemeral, symbolic feature in nature as the focus of our restoration efforts — not the processes that had created such a feature. The essence of ecological design is the establishment of sustainable, resilient natural processes that will support natural wonders. It is not the design of the wonders themselves. What was at issue was a way of living with nature, rather than imposing one's will on it. Once the processes are right and adequate space is provided for nature to adapt, the indicators of a healthy, thriving ecological system will return as a dynamic balance is reestablished under the new set of circumstances. This error by a group of individuals at the forefront of the ecological-design movement reflected the depth of misunderstanding within our culture about living with healthy wild nature. We thought we knew what we were doing, but we were stuck in an old paradigm, seduced by an image of nature as something we should control, rather than trusting in the natural process to create the conditions for the iconic image to evolve in its own way and in its own time.

Armed with the new insights about the watershed and humbled by our collective design arrogance, the project was restarted in the mid-1990s and led to a different conclusion about the restoration of diverse habitats at Muir Beach. We would no longer attempt to re-create Big Lagoon. Instead, we would create the conditions for a natural stream channel to meander across a reestablished floodplain, helping to transport

Redwood Creek breaches to the ocean after the first winter storms, inviting salmon into the watershed and children to play. 2013. JNRA.

sediments to the ocean rather than depositing them in a manmade lagoon. Areas for resting salmon, turtles, and frogs would be included in what would become a restored natural coastal creek. And, in anticipation of a future rise in sea level as a result of climate change and global warming, its backwater areas would be further conceived of as one day being able to accommodate higher water levels and the potential for a natural reestablishment of Big Lagoon.

The parking lot, restrooms, picnic areas, and trailhead have today also all been relocated to prior disturbed areas near the Muir Beach residential developments, with minimal intrusion into the wetlands. The big move here was to rotate the parking lot, which formerly cut straight across the floodplain, so that it was tucked to the side of the wetlands, allowing the creek to meander freely. This also means that visitors look directly toward the ocean across the beach and a small remnant tidal lagoon when they enter the park. The new alignment thus allows them to see the beach as the main destination, but also to be aware of

its whole coastal context. The experience of this place is designed to be more than simply an ocean beach.

The journey to the beach from the parking lot is also not direct. It takes the visitor first on a 430-foot-long pedestrian bridge over the restored floodplain, wetlands, and creek through alder and willow groves. Slightly above and separated from the sensitive areas for protection from human intrusion, visitors thus experience the wetland habitat before arriving at the dunes and beach. On the opposite end of the bridge the wholly accessible path then joins the Coastal Trail, traversing restored sand dunes before opening out to the beach itself. By design the new route allows visitors to come into contact with wild nature — an experience that will become part of their memories of this place and serve as a point of reference for future encounters with nature.

The wild coho salmon that have spawned in Redwood Creek for millennia have today been greatly reduced in number. Where once there were tens of thousands, fewer than 100 individuals were found in a recent count. In a heroic effort, wild offspring were collected in 2014 from the stream and raised in a nearby hatchery before being released into Redwood Creek to spawn. That effort to jumpstart a robust new salmon run appears to have produced a good number of healthy offspring, and there is reason to hope those fish will return at the end of their three-year ocean adventure to spawn a new generation. But the cohorts from the yearly cycles in between do not appear to be doing as well. An extended drought, warmer weather, and increased disease could be contributing factors. Only time will tell.

In the meantime, when you go to Muir Beach in the future, look for osprey soaring in the sky. They are voracious feeders on fresh fish and haven't been seen much in the Muir Beach area for decades. But the conditions are now ripe for their return. Ospreys need clear water and abundant fish to thrive and are an indicator of healthy waterways and diverse wetland habitats. If you see them, you will know that the restored ecosystem is healthy once again. With a bit of luck and enlightened management, the wild coho salmon that once filled Redwood Creek will be a part of the mix and we'll know that the coho re-wilding is working. ⊛

Right page: The journey to the beach leads across the creek to the Coastal Trail and through the dunes. 2016. Hanh Nguyen.
Following page: Redwood Creek's watershed, restored tidal lagoon and floodplain, and bridge hidden within the trees at Muir Beach. 2021. JNRA.

INTERWOVEN IN THE FOREST FLOOR

MUIR WOODS NATIONAL MONUMENT
Frank Valley Road at Muir Woods Road
Mill Valley, CA

Right page: Nearing sunset in the old growth redwoods of Muir Woods. Jose Luis Aranda.

In the name of protection of individual iconic trees for the pleasure of an ever-increasing number of visitors, the critically important forest network was being seriously damaged.

During the early days after I established my own office, between trips to the post office, hanging out at the public tennis courts, helping Jody with her children's theater troupe, and teaching at UC Extension, I was invited to assist an architect in the siting of a new visitor center for Muir Woods National Monument. I knew the park and park conservancy staff, and they had recommended that the architect contact me. This unexpected referral was the beginning of a fruitful decades-long association with Muir Woods.

The architect had designed a beautiful, small building for greeting visitors and organizing ranger tours that also housed a little bookstore, but he and the park staff were unsure exactly where to locate it. Until that time, there was no visitor-contact facility at the monument, only a bathroom near the entry road and a small ranger station with a food service concession deep within the forest. The parking lot was also crowded all the way up to the edge of the forest, and the main visitor connection to the trails was obscured by overgrown vegetation and cars. While searching for the giant coast redwood trees, most visitors, instead of walking along the trail, would mistakenly walk up the service road to the maintenance area. Our charge was to locate a new building so as to create a clear point of entry to greet and orient visitors without disturbing the nature of the place.

Choosing to displace asphalt rather than vegetation, we sited the new building in the portion of the parking lot closest to the forest. A big leaf maple tree had been planted directly in front of the path to the forest years before as a way to mark its location, but instead of showing the way in, it effectively blocked it. To frame the entry space while blocking views of the service road, we thus transplanted this tree to a new planting bed beside the building and filled the planting area with native trees and understory shrubs found at margins of coast redwood forests. This allowed the creation of an informal but spacious entry plaza on the creek side of the building, with open views of the creek, benches, and a re-created historic gateway arch and sign readily legible to all visitors. The new entry focused the attention of visitors on the first stand of redwood trees while revealing the ecological context for the forest.

Beyond the entry, visitors walked into a majestic enclosed old-growth forest, where shafts of light penetrate the dark interior between the powerful trunks of the giant trees. And when their eyes adjust to the lower light levels, they begin to see the subtle complexities of not just the awe inspiring vertical forms, but also the rich forest understory. The return trip to the parking lot, however, brought a jarring transition from dark to light, without spatial relief. Immediately upon leaving the forest, with their eyes adjusted to the forest darkness, people would be blinded by sunlight reflecting off the vehicles parked there. To allow people to transition out of the forest experience more gracefully, I recommended that the innermost parking lot be removed and replaced with a transitional savannah-like landscape. My unsolicited advice, accompanied by a simple diagram, was taken to heart by the staff. But it took twenty-plus years for this parking lot to be mostly removed. The large, rustic, plaza-like space that occupies this apace today serves as an active community gathering area and forecourt to the magnificent forest.

Removal of the innermost parking lot solved another seemingly intractable problem for the park staff. As the parking lot nearest to the forest, it was the one most visitors wanted to use, even though it was relatively small. Convenience was paramount, and since the parking was offered, it was aggressively pursued, to the point where virtually every day people would get into fights over the spaces there. Tempers flared so frequently that armed park police were required to be on site at all times to control the violence. This was not the kind of experience the National Park Service felt should be offered to visitors. But the simple act of eliminating the inner parking lot and requiring visitors to walk a short distance to the entry effectively solved the problem. The more distant lots were more equitable, with no privileged close-in spaces. And getting people out of their cars to walk along the short trail to the entry helped dissipate the pent-up frustrations caused by the circuitous road to the site. Along the pathway from the lots visitors were also made aware of the context of the redwood forest, providing a more compelling introduction to it as well as a decompression zone after the experience. Since that time, most of the parking lots have been moved even further away from the entry, to lots served by a shuttle system. And reservations are now required to visit Muir Woods, effectively controlling congestion and limiting the number of visitors in the narrow valley.

The forecourt to Muir Woods has significantly improved the visitor arrival experience by providing spatial relief and revealing the broader landscape context of the forest. But accessible parking and service vehicles still occupy a significant portion of the space — a continuing imposition of our automotive culture on what should be a vehicle-free landscape and ecological transition zone. As the redwood forest heals and we increasingly nurture whole natural systems, the boundary between the redwoods and the adjacent woodlands will and should become less distinct over time. The remaining vehicles should be removed from this area while still meeting accessibility standards — or at the least, they should be subsumed within an expanded mixed evergreen woodland and screened from view.

Such a reconceptualization of Muir Woods has been a long time coming. For years, the number of visitors in the narrow park had been increasing exponentially while the health of the forest had been deteriorating. Indeed, for most of its early decades as a national monument, visitors were allowed to walk (and even drive) anywhere they chose within the forest. The elite Bohemian Club, composed of influential men from the San Francisco area, even claimed one of the groves for their raucous annual gathering and regraded it to make it more hospitable for their tents. Understory vegetation was removed and replaced with lawns, the then-popular Algerian Ivy, and other invasive exotic plants. The effect was to make the place more familiar to visitors, but less habitable for native plants and animals.

Right page: View of the new Visitor Contact Station at the forest entry shortly after opening with the relocated Big Leaf Maple tree to the side. 1986. NPS.

The boardwalk placed visitors in a special position slightly above the forest floor to protect the intertwined roots and soils while allowing people to feel closely connected with the setting.

To make matters worse, the naturally meandering Redwood Creek was straightened, cleared of snags and forest litter, and its banks were armored with stone riprap in a misguided effort to protect trees that had survived without intervention for thousands of years. Changes to the creek further destroyed spawning pools and riffles, causing the collapse of the southernmost population of wild coho salmon on the West Coast. Meanwhile, trees that died and fell to the ground were routinely removed to keep the forest floor clean and neat. As a result, a self-sustaining continuum between life and death, with fallen trees and litter becoming living soils supporting commingled roots, was broken, and the forest began to die. In the name of protecting individual, iconic trees for the pleasure of an ever-increasing number of visitors, a critically important forest network was seriously damaged.

By the late 1960s evidence of the forest's decline could no longer be ignored, and its managers began to change their policies. Arguments within the park hierarchy about the fate of fallen trees would now be decided in favor of the health of the system, allowing forest litter and fallen giants to be left in place to complete their full life cycle, blurring the artificial distinction between life and death. A nursery was created to grow plants indigenous to Muir Woods to reestablish native understory habitats. Exotic, invasive vegetation was systematically removed. And to better control visitor access and protect the root systems from unfettered trampling, the park installed asphalt pathways and low fences. But those pathways, too, proved insufficient in the most heavily trafficked areas, as the trees still suffered stress as a result of soil compaction and the lack of air, water, and nutrients to replenish the soils beneath them. It had become clear that reestablishing the health of the forest floor, with its network of intertwined roots, was the key to protecting the trees.

Shortly after the visitor center was installed in the 1980s, the park began to remove the asphalt paths in select areas and replace them with elevated boardwalks. To protect the forest floor in the most heavily affected areas, we designed a wholly accessible system of elevated trails and gathering areas with interpretive displays. The boardwalks here were made of recycled redwood boards from abandoned warehouses from the Northern

Left page: Elevated boardwalks allow visitors to experience the forest while protecting the interwoven tree roots. 2016. Hanh Nguyen.

Restored, healthy ecological systems can thrive side by side with carefully considered public access even in one of the most heavily visited places in the entire National Park system.

California coast. And, instead of railings to keep people on them, we placed simple wood curbs at their edges. The boardwalks now help protect the intertwined roots and soils below, while placing visitors in a special position slightly above the forest floor but still closely connected with the setting. The success of the boardwalks for both visitors and the forest has since led to their extension into other locations of heavy visitor impact, as well as to a succession of broader public access changes. These today include parking alterations and shuttle/transportation options, roadway redesign, trail linkages, service/nursery expansion, and a reservation system for all visitors.

The combination of all these efforts has improved both the health of the forest and the experience of Muir Woods for millions of visitors each year. The roots of trees are once again communicating with each other. The creek's natural meanders are being restored. The native understory vegetation is thriving with measurable improvements to natural habitats and diversity of wildlife. Northern spotted owls are returning, and conditions have been reestablished for a return of native coho salmon and steelhead trout. Muir Woods has demonstrated that restored, healthy ecological systems can thrive side by side with carefully considered public access, even in one of the most heavily visited sites in the entire U.S. National Park system. ⊛

Right page: Redwood Creek is once again supporting spawning Coho salmon and Steelhead trout after decades of decline. 2019. Jose Luis Aranda.

Page 116: The wholly accessible elevated boardwalk and gathering areas manage public access while protecting the giant trees and the restored habitat. 2016. Hanh Nguyen.

South Bay Counties

PRIDE OF PLACE

POCO WAY NEIGHBORHOOD REVITALIZATION
Poco Way at McCreery Ave, north of Story Road
Near confluence of the 101 and 680 Freeways
San Jose, CA

Right page: The once dangerous and decrepit San Jose neighborhood was transformed into a place of dignity and pride. Before, 1992. JNRA.

By participating in its creation, the
residents would be more invested
in the place and inclined to take
responsibility for it once completed.
We were creating homes for real
people and helping to build a
community, not just a housing
development.

P oco Way was a place where you lived only if you had no other options. It
was a block and a half of constant gang activity, gunfire, drug dealing,
prostitution, and street violence near downtown San Jose. Outsiders
rarely visited, and then only if they were looking for trouble or dope. Its smelly, decrepit,
rat-infested, and burnt-out two-story buildings were home to the poorest of the poor
immigrants hoping for a better life in California. Vietnamese, Cambodian, and Central
and South American families were the principal tenants, with as many as twenty people
sometimes living in a single apartment next door to gang members and drug dealers. Easy
direct access from Poco Way, a semi-secluded side street with fast getaway routes to either
of two freeways, served the drug trade well as a place of business. At the time we became
involved in a project there it had become a magnet for violence, being the site of more
drive-by shootings than any other place in California.

These conditions all changed in the early 1990s when, in a coordinated,
community-driven effort, local housing officials, educators, community groups, police,
firefighters, elected officials, and recreation managers all committed themselves and
their institutions to transform the place. They organized and collectively forced out the
dangerous criminal activities while framing a vision of a future built around community
protection, a rejuvenated physical environment, and pride of place.

Once committed to transforming the Poco Way neighborhood, with financing
in hand, the city began to search for a design team that could envision how its badly
deteriorated built environment could be reconceived. I was hired by the San Jose Housing
Authority as part of a team led by Herman Stoller Coliver Architects that was ultimately
charged with redesigning the place. The work would require reenvisioning buildings and
outdoor spaces, as both were contributors to the inhumane living conditions. Yet we also
understood that, while physical changes were essential, the real long-term success of the
project would depend upon the ongoing support of a variety of government agencies and a
commitment by the community to take control of its own destiny. But an improved built
environment could provide a critical foundation for the families who would be living there
while creating a proud symbol of hard-won changes underway.

One of our first acts of placemaking was to conduct a series of workshops with
the people who lived at Poco Way to determine how they thought about the place and
what they would like to see in their newly conceived homes. It was important to us as a
design team, and to the San Jose Housing Authority as the owner of the facility, to create
an entirely new place that reflected the values of the people who would be living there.
By participating in its creation, the residents would become more invested in it and more
inclined to take responsibility for it once completed. We saw our role as creating homes
for real people and helping to build a community, not just producing another subsidized
housing environment.

What was once a place of terror
and despair is now a place of hope,
pride, and dignity. But the physical
improvements are only part of the
story. One can forget what it took to
make such a place, and what it takes to
sustain it. And if the story is forgotten,
the place can be gone in an instant.

Translators for the Vietnamese-, Cambodian-, and Spanish-speaking tenants were required for the workshops. Most of the participants had never met an architect, much less had anyone ask them how they might envision their homes or their gardens. Initially, cautious responses to intimate questions about cooking arrangements, for instance, or bedrooms began to reveal important cultural cues to the design of the buildings. But once they were convinced that their input was essential for the design, people began to speak up more confidently, and the discussion broadened to reveal how families interact spatially in different cultures. The outcome was an architectural proposal that embodied a mix of subtly varied housing types that addressed the range of cultural preferences among the people living there. As a result of these discussions, more than 85 percent of the people who had lived there before the effort began returned to live in the places that they helped to conceive.

The residents had as much to say about the outdoor spaces at Poco Way as they did about the buildings. Most had been raised in rural areas and as both an economic necessity and a cultural preference were interested in growing their own food. Since almost anything would grow in the San Jose climate, a young Salvadoran woman asked if the common areas could have orange trees. Yes, it could, was my immediate reply. But the maintenance staff vehemently objected, saying that if fruit were grown there, people would throw it against the buildings. Fortunately, the Housing Authority's project manager quickly and forcefully responded that surely fruit was far less lethal than the bullets from the Uzi machine guns these people had been living with for years. Most of the fruit would be eaten anyway. Orange, lemon, and other fruit and nut trees were subsequently planted throughout the complex.

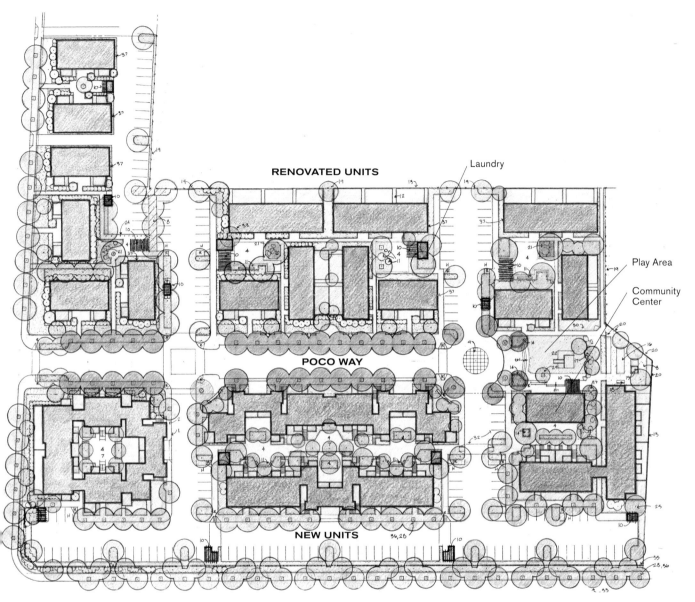

Site plan showing blocked-off Poco Way with play area, interlinked courtyards, and lush landscape. 1995. JNRA.

With information from the tenants and managers in hand, we began our process of reimagining how the spaces could be altered to allow people to live safely and comfortably in this place and build a sense of community. Our combined analysis concluded that half the burnt-out buildings were fundamentally sound, and that with thoughtful redesign they could be salvaged and reconceived as warm, welcoming structures grouped in new arrangements around a series of interconnected courtyards. The remaining buildings would be removed and replaced with new building clusters and courtyard gardens. The buildings to be removed would be those that were in worse shape or that were configured in ways that were not conducive to the creation of courtyards or the implementation of other community-building actions. In every case, new building entries would be designed to integrate with new gardens and activate the courtyards, incorporating front stoops so people could sit outside and share a sense of common space. The most important goals throughout the site were to address security issues, create a safer environment, establish resident control over the spaces, and create a sense of common community. The creation of shared courtyards was integral to all these.

One of the most important things we learned during our site observations was that redesigning the communal laundries in each of the building clusters was critical to creating a safe environment. Originally located at the end of dead-end pathways, these

Poco Way has become a place to raise a family and nurture community bonds. 2001. JNRA.

were particularly dangerous places. The women who did the family laundry could be easily trapped in the laundries by aggressors, and, without means of escape, they were routinely assaulted there. We saw abject terror in the women's faces as they carried heavy loads of laundry down the pathways. While women were particularly vulnerable, these dead-end pathways were also conducive to violent acts in general. It became clear that if we could eliminate the dead-ends, anyone being threatened would at least have a second means of escape. It also became clear that if the laundries were to be relocated to the front entrances to the courtyards, they could function as control points for residents. The women who most frequented them might even then be empowered to become the eyes and ears of the courtyard and gain a measure of control over who entered these semi-private spaces. The reconceived site plans thus eliminated the dead-ends and instead established a series of interconnected pedestrian courtyards. The laundries were also all relocated to the courtyard entries and equipped with direct telecommunication lines to the security office.

The street, Poco Way, had originally been a short through-street, and its open-ended configuration had allowed drug dealers to drive in, make their deals, and race out the other end. Closing the street to through-traffic was another design move that we saw as essential to creating a safer place. Our solution was to block off the street and reclaim it for use by the residents by placing a large pile of dirt at its far end, locating a children's play area on top of it, and constructing a community center building next to it. Poco Way, formerly a through-road/raceway, was thus transformed into a cul-de-sac terminating at the main community gathering space for the neighborhood — a space dedicated to children and families.

Another important step we took was to narrow the street itself and reconceive it as a shaded, tree-lined promenade fronted by stoops and second-floor balconies. The

The creation of shared courtyards was a central strategy to create a safer environment, to establish control over the spaces, and to create a community commons.

"eyes on the street" provided by the residents of adjoining units might thus prove critical to reclaiming the neighborhood, maintaining security, and creating a sense of community. Meanwhile, the narrowed cul-de-sac street in combination with a new broad sidewalk promenade could be reconceived as a central landscape commons for the neighborhood. To this new space the community's Hispanic residents could also bring their heritage of *paseando*, according to which neighbors, parents, grandparents, and children meet daily to walk around a central common area. In the past, Poco Way had simply been too dangerous to allow for the continuation of this practice from their Latin American hometowns, and young people had congregated in the nearby schoolyard instead. But the well-tended, lushly planted street and sidewalk, closed to through traffic and over which people look from neighboring apartments, has now been reclaimed as a community promenade where young and old strut their stuff, to see and be seen as part of the theater of daily life.

Following page: Concrete round benches separate an auto court from the gardens and serve the gathering area. 2016. JNRA.

As part of our analysis of the place we also discovered that Cambodian men liked to gather in groups in shaded semi-public outdoor spaces away from peering eyes to play cards, gamble, or simply to visit and watch the action. Once we understood the need for this kind of activity, we massaged the extremely confined site plan to create opportunities for such informal semi-public spaces. Much to our surprise, we found an unusual but perfectly acceptable solution that also brought cultures together. The new buildings were conceived around a series of garden courtyards that would open to the street promenade beneath small "tuck-under" parking areas. The parking areas formed a seamless open space transition

between the garden courts and the public street/promenade, and, since the people parking in those prime spots rarely moved their cars, they became informal gathering areas. We also modified the shaded "tuck-under" areas to include concrete seating and game tables that would double as vehicular barriers to the courtyards, giving the promenade an unexpected cultural extension.

When the construction was finally finished and Poco Way was reopened for the residents, the city held a grand opening celebration with endless speeches by politicians and dignitaries. Jody and I attended. The audience was mostly composed of professional

people and others associated with the multiple agencies and interest groups that had made the project possible. The ceremony was at the new community center, and Poco Way itself was lined with empty tables. The police and fire department brought in a giant barbeque and cooked hot dogs and hamburgers. When the last speech was finally over, the residents began streaming out of their apartments onto the sidewalks, where they filled the tables with foods from each of their cultures made specially for the occasion. While most of the immigrant children preferred the American hot dogs and hamburgers, Jody and I feasted on delicious homemade Vietnamese, Cambodian, and Latin American dishes. We were later invited by several of the residents to tour their new apartments and gardens, which they proudly opened for outsiders to see. When the project first started, the Housing Authority would not allow me to visit the site after 10 AM each morning. After that time, when the drug dealers and gang members began to stir, it was simply too dangerous for an outsider. Now, the residents wanted to share their homes with pride.

The large public investment in Poco Way resulted in a beautiful, responsive, and beloved new built environment. The physical transformation created a safe place to live, to nurture families, and to build community bonds. People now love living in this place. What had once been a place of terror and despair was transformed into one of hope, pride, and dignity. Poco Way now provides a home for 128 very poor and mostly immigrant families, and there is a long waiting list to get in. The physical changes were extensive, subtle, and enduring, and they have done about as much as possible to create a positive foundation for the neighborhood to flourish. But the physical improvements are only part of the story. The challenge from the moment it was completed — and one that continues today — has been to maintain a commitment to the community and sustain the mutual support that was nurtured during the design process. It is fragile. People must continue looking out for each other, take care of their homes, and honor their shared spaces. One can forget what it took to make such a place, and what it takes to sustain it. And if the story is forgotten, the positive attributes of this place may be wiped away in an instant. ⊚

Right page: Shared garden courtyards are interlinked, creating a lush and safe community commons, 2012. JNRA.

JUST THE PLACE FOR AN ICE-CREAM SOCIAL

MERCY BUSH NEIGHBORHOOD PARK
Mercy and Bush Streets (Near downtown)
Mountain View, CA

Right page: A hidden pathway meanders within a riparian forest along the dry stream bed. 2021. Jose Luis Aranda.

There was a clear sense of community but, until Mercy Bush Park was built, there was no nearby common area in which to gather.

F amilies with small children in the Old Mountain View neighborhood of modest single family homes, big trees, and quiet streets near downtown Mountain View wanted and needed a neighborhood park. But their concerns had long been bypassed in favor of the development of newer residential areas. This is the story of how ordinary people came together to create a community commons for their neighborhood.

This neighborhood is at the historic core of the city, the last remnant of a small-scale rural town from an earlier time. The agricultural fields and orchards that once lay just outside the neighborhood in this fertile valley are gone today, entirely displaced by suburban housing tracts, office parks, broad collector streets, and freeways. The change began when Mountain View became ground zero for the growth of what would be known as Silicon Valley, center of the global high-tech industry. As money flowed in and enriched the city's coffers, the old downtown was renovated to reflect the town's new image of itself. Growth became rampant. Fancy new shops and restaurants complemented expensive urban-design improvements along Castro Street. Property values skyrocketed, and many of the modest homes throughout the city were transformed into impressive new structures.

The neighbors in Old Mountain View, however, liked their neighborhood and fought to maintain its character. They valued the small-town feel, the sense of the history in the place, and the quirky jogs in the streets that make drivers slow down and let neighbors get to know each other. There was a clear sense of community within this area, but until Mercy Bush Park was built, there was no common area in which to gather. Groups of people would get together occasionally at each other's houses for weekend barbecues and other festivities, but they wanted a real public park. Eventually, when a house and two adjacent lots came up for sale at the corner of Mercy and Bush Streets, the neighbors pressured the city council to buy the properties and commit to building a park there. The city staff objected, arguing that an upgrade to a nearby mini-park should be satisfactory. But the city council did finally agree to purchase the 2/3-acre site — even if it would then take almost ten more years for the empty lots to be transformed into the park the city had promised.

The city staff in Mountain View was not accustomed to well-organized community groups influencing its agenda. The Park and Recreation Department functioned with considerable autonomy and in their own time frame, having grown accustomed to large budgets and the general quiescence of the citizenry. The staff had created a wonderful park system, which largely reflected their vision of what parks should be, and the city's residents generally enjoyed what was offered. The activists in Old Mountain View, on the other hand, became increasingly frustrated with the city's delay in converting the lots it had purchased into a park. And after three years without progress, residents of the area organized themselves to design a park on their own with the assistance of students from nearby San Jose State University. The students then created a plan for the park, and the neighbors returned to the city to ask it to build what they had designed.

The city staff was in a bind. The plan developed by the students was unconstrained by fiscal or engineering realities. Yet it was the product of a stimulating process, and it reflected the neighborhood goals. As laudable student work, it might provide a good point of beginning. But the student plan was clearly not sufficient for a public agency to act on, and the city staff awkwardly continued to dismiss it, no matter how creative it appeared. Undeterred, the neighborhood persisted in its appeals to elected officials. And after a few more years of incessant pressure, the effort finally paid off when the mayor and city council established a budget for the project and instructed the staff to design a park on the lots at Mercy and Bush Streets.

It was at this point that I was hired to help develop plans for the park — but more importantly, to serve as a buffer between the city staff and the neighborhood. I had successfully designed two parks previously for the city, so the staff knew and trusted me. I also had a track record of projects designed through a community-outreach process. The community's leaders were thus comforted that their voices might be heard, even though they had not been allowed to participate in the consultant selection process. To begin, I was given a week by the staff to do a detailed critique of the student/neighborhood plan. The staff's stated expectation was that I would declare the plans to have minimal merit; they assumed I would dismiss the work and design the park as they envisioned it. But my response was not what they expected. When I saw the plans, I chose to affirm what the neighbors had accomplished, validate their perceptions, and build upon the process they had started. I determined that their considerable energy was a positive force that could be harnessed to drive the project toward a meaningful conclusion.

I culled the insights, desires, wish lists, and ideas from the plans they had developed and used their perceptions as a basis for our first meeting. Staff expected twenty people to show up and were astonished when more than 75 arrived. They were overwhelmed at the amount of interest in the project. Through their sheer number and interest, the citizens had clearly taken control of the process. The staff stepped behind the shield of their consultant and hoped for the best. The meeting had been scheduled for one hour, but it lasted four. There was a lot to discuss. Five years had passed, and it was important for the neighbors to revisit their thinking, hear from new residents of the area, and consider what might have changed over time. But simple validation of the creative work they had already done fundamentally changed the dynamic of the project. They felt empowered, and it stimulated them to want to contribute to this new direction the project was taking. They were also looking for guidance from me. For their part, the staff was silent for the entire evening but relieved to see the momentum shift from antagonism to engagement.

When I was able to offer a reasoned critique of the design proposals developed by the neighbors, it opened a broader discussion about parks, spatial design, public/private uses, cultural heritage, construction methodology, and budget realities. The rich exchange

The simple validation of the creative work that they had already done fundamentally changed the dynamic of the project. They were empowered and stimulated to contribute to this new undertaking. This was the essence of Community Design.

energized the entire group. The neighbors were activists who were not trained in the work of placemaking, but they knew that with enlightened and respectful guidance, they could make a special place that would be meaningful to them. At the initial meeting people also offered insights about how they lived, the spaces they wished to inhabit, the kind of spaces in which they felt comfortable interacting with neighbors, and the characteristics of their neighborhood and city. The range of sensual pleasures derived from a landscape were important to many, and all agreed on the need for a common space in which to meet neighbors and raise their children. The comments were personal, and everyone spoke — young people and adults, shy and outspoken people, women, and men. Over the course of the meeting people found common ground as they came to know each other more deeply.

The relationship between client and designer is most intimate. This is a necessary and complex part of most landscape and architectural design processes since our work is to create spaces for everyday lives of ordinary people. This would be their park. And the essence of community design is that I needed to listen attentively and design their park responsively. As people spoke, various physical/spatial responses began swirling around in my mind. Since my next visit with the neighbors would be with alternative plans for the park, I could not help but begin formulating design concepts that might tie the many insights together into coherent whole.

Some neighbors were drawn to open, clearly ordered, simply organized, and easily understood spaces with everything in its proper place. Others reveled in richly textured informal spaces in which they could invent their own activities. Several remembered joyous stories of farm life in family orchards. These insights would structure the park design options we would develop for the next workshop. The neighbors were also very clear that

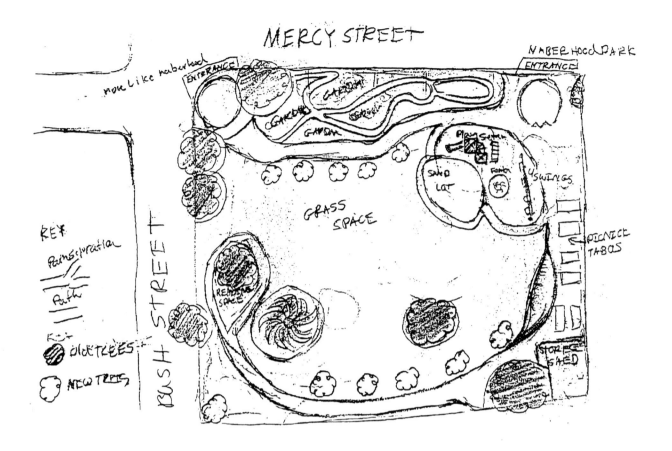

Plan prepared by 13-year old Amy Davis at the community workshop became the basis of the final park plans. 2000. Amy Davis

education had to be a key component of their park, and so educational messages would need to be woven into the composition of the place. In addition, the keen interest in basic science and math expressed by many led me to imagine Euclidean and fractal geometries as spatial organizational principles corresponding with the cultural and natural heritage of the place.

As the meeting closed, I was approached by Amy Davis, a thirteen-year-old who had been an active participant the entire evening. She gave me a drawing she had done while the discussions were underway. It was actually two drawings: a palimpsest, with one plan for the park, generally to scale, that she had drawn during the meeting, and another that she had superimposed over it in response to comments from her neighbors. Her drawing was clear, proportionally accurate, exuberant, and instinctively responsive to both the site and the comments she had heard. It showed a surprising sophistication in its spatial arrangement. And it reflected her own inventive use of the site as an adventure play area while growing up. That precocious young girl felt empowered to share her ideas — a reflection of her own strength of

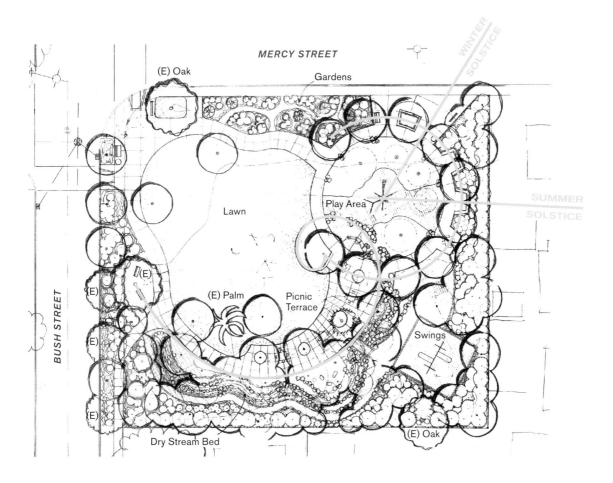

Park Master Plan approved by the community for construction with interlocking geometries highlighted. 2000. JNRA.

The ecological orderliness and spatial complexity incorporated the essential features from Amy Davis' sketch.

character, the supportive parenting and home-schooling she had received, and the inclusive nature of the design process we had begun. I determined right then that Amy's plan would inform one of the two options we brought back to the neighbors.

The alternative park designs that I subsequently developed for a follow-up workshop faithfully reflected the information received at the initial meeting, but they reflected two very different kinds of places that could be created. One scheme was laid out with a formal orchard-like arrangement of trees as a counterpoint to the placement

Following page: The Park is a neighborhood oasis where people of all ages meet on a regular basis. 2021. Jose Luis Aranda.

of recreational features. It was an orderly, minimalist scheme with everything in its place within a spacious and clear geometric arrangement that reflected both the agricultural heritage of the area and the city's new modernist urban-design imagery. The other scheme was organized organically around a boulder-strewn natural stream channel that would serve as an adventure play feature. This would unwind through the park in a Fibonacci spiral, juxtaposed against a Euclidian circular form containing a more standard play structure. This more informal arrangement also used natural California landscape ecology to structure a "wild" and less predictable experience of place. The ecological orderliness and spatial complexity of this arrangement was not as familiar to most people as the more cultivated urban landscape of the other scheme. Yet this scheme incorporated the essential features from Amy Davis's sketch — although that was not revealed to the group.

The weight of opinion among the neighbors at the second meeting initially settled on the geometric scheme. Its familiar graphic clarity represented the common idea of what a designed space should be. But after considerable back and forth, those attending began to understand the subtleties of the second scheme. It provided more area for the uses they valued most, more variety among small- and larger-scale spaces, more spatial mystery, an experiential education about the ecology of place, more informal exploration than proscribed use, and a reflection of natural heritage more than cultural adaptations. At the beginning of the evening, only one person had expressed interest in the second scheme. But as people began to understand the second scheme better, they found themselves more comfortable with it. And by the end of the evening, the assembly of neighbors was unanimous in its choice of the second option, much to the disappointment of the city staff.

After the group voted to codify their choice and to communicate their preference to the city council and the mayor, I showed them the plan that Amy Davis had drawn at the first meeting and compared it with the plan that they had chosen. The source of the chosen plan was clear to all, and quite a surprise to Amy and her family. The design for the park that would be built, guided by a professional committed to community design, had come from the people themselves. They had organized so successfully they had created their own neighborhood park. It was theirs, and they would nourish and protect it.

In the end, the park at Mercy and Bush Streets was built within the established budget and was filled with people as soon as it opened. It now serves as a public garden, a play facility for local children, a picnic area for families, a place of exploration and adventure, a place for ice cream socials, a place to learn about solstice alignments and Fibonacci spirals, and a place to simply relax in nature with friends. It is a simple, comfortable, beautiful place conceived by those who could see a need, and it was composed by someone who could help them make their vision a reality. It did not exist before, but it now is central to the identity of a neighborhood. ⊙

Left page: Water play in the play area leads to an intermittent stream bed and native habitat for adventure exploration unfolding in a Fibonacci spiral. 2021. Jose Luis Aranda.

LIVING WITH DEATH

COLMA HISTORICAL PARK AND COMMUNITY CENTER
1520 Hillside Boulevard
Colma, CA

Right page: The park, anchored by a historic museum and the funeral train station, is the place for community gatherings and children's play. 2021. JNRA.

This is a place where the cycle of life is celebrated openly and without fear, blurred into a continuum of beginnings and endings and beginnings again, past and future memories, each contributing to the experience of now.

The Town of Colma is a place that houses the dead. It achieved this status when San Francisco's cemeteries were all relocated there in the early twentieth century during the city's westward expansion following the 1906 earthquake. As the Bay Area's necropolis, Colma today has some 2,000 living residents but more than 1.5 million dead people buried in seventeen cemeteries (and an unknown number of animals buried in one pet cemetery). Funeral processions, burials, tending to the cemetery grounds, and overseeing the ritual passage between life and death are the jobs that engage virtually all the citizens of the town. As a part of the natural cycle of life, Colma residents live honorably with death every day, passing the cemeteries on their way to the grocery store, while taking children to school, or walking to the park. The citizens fully embrace the unique identity of their place. They take great pride in their work facilitating passage from one state of being to the next.

As the cemeteries grew over the years, so too did the town — but much more slowly. The business of death never ends, but the number of people who choose to answer the calling of this business is more limited. As a result, the small, tight-knit community of this place never managed to build a central public space to serve its own needs. The manicured grounds of the cemeteries created a beautiful landscape, but the cemeteries themselves were private and not available for community use. The people needed their own public gathering space, one that would allow them to celebrate together, interact with neighbors, and strengthen their common bonds.

The site they eventually chose for their commons was near their one residential neighborhood, on a west-facing hillside, overlooking the verdant valley, and surrounded by lushly planted cemeteries on all four sides. Embedded deeply within and linked inextricably with the necropolis, it provided a setting that resonated with the community. This place had once served as a part of the main ceremonial entry for one of the older cemeteries, but that entry had recently been moved to another location. Nevertheless, the old gateway building still stood. It had been designated a State Historic Resource, and the cemetery had agreed to donate it to the town so it could be converted to a town history museum. The seed for a larger community space reflecting the unique heritage of this place had been planted.

With the museum in place, plans for a larger complex soon developed in a way that would emphasize the proud cultural origins of the town. Anchored by the museum, this complex would include a new community center building, a historic funeral train station, a hillside promenade, a grassy lawn, a picnic area, gardens, and interpretive features. The site would be designed with an austere dignity consistent with the town's vision of the work of its citizenry. The new community center building was designed to complement the Spanish Colonial Revival style of the historic gatehouse/museum and was located at the far southern end of the site, directly overlooking and adjacent to the Jewish and Italian cemeteries. A palm-lined promenade then linked the community center and museum to one another along

Following page: The Community Center and Historic Park is located on a hillside overlooking the verdant valley and surrounded by cemeteries, the town's business. 2019. Jose Luis Aranda.

the top of the hill, offering views across the valley and to the cemeteries above and below. The promenade was envisioned as a place for processions, formal events, and for interpreting the town's history. A historic funeral train station and tracks were moved to a site alongside it, with a series of gardens commemorating the war dead from the town itself. On its other side, a lawn sloped down to a family picnic area and terrace overlooking the Italian cemetery. The entire park might thus provide a place of reflection and community memory, as well as for townspeople to come together in celebrations of life.

Within the orderly structure of this place, the people of the town now make full use of the open space for lively activities of their own invention. An impromptu motocross course around the central lawn may transform into a pickup soccer field, and then into a place to meet friends or engage in quiet exploration. It offers a rich, multilayered landscape experience in an extraordinary setting. This is a place where the cycle of life is celebrated openly and without fear, blurred into a continuum of beginnings and endings and beginnings again, past and future memories, each contributing to the experience of now. ⊕

Napa & Sonoma Counties

REDISCOVERING THE ORIGINS OF A RIVER TOWN

PETALUMA RIVER ACCESS AND ENHANCEMENT PLAN
Petaluma, CA

Right page: The river greenway is the lifeblood of the town, linking together farm fields, residential areas, river-related agri-industrial complexes, the commercial downtown, and downstream salt marshes. 2021. Jose Luis Aranda.

The key to its economic resurgence would be an ecologically responsible reclamation of its river corridor and the downtown river frontage in particular.

For ten thousand years the place called Petaluma in the Coast Miwok language has supported communities of people along the banks of a slow-moving river. Today a small city is located there. However, long before the arrival of Europeans, Native people lived just upstream from its future downtown, where they enjoyed access to fresh drinking water, rich tidal marshes, and abundant wildlife in the surrounding grasslands and woodlands. Trading in local resources was common with neighboring tribes (for obsidian flints from nearby Clear Lake, for instance). They were a people living along the river in harmony with the natural environment, whose prosperity was part of the long heritage of the place.

Legend has it that, in the mid- to late nineteenth century, a couple of drunken sailors brought their boat as far upstream on Petaluma Creek as they could before running aground at a large meander. Their abandoned boat thus marked the place from which, at high tide, it was possible to navigate the thirteen miles downstream to San Pablo Bay, and from there to the booming city of San Francisco. A new port was born at this site to serve the rich agricultural lands of west Marin and southern Sonoma Counties. Soon, roads extended like spokes in a wheel from what would become the downtown Petaluma waterfront to the remotest parts of the surrounding farmlands. And a thriving commercial center with a burgeoning population eventually developed around the waterfront warehouses and docks, the lifeblood of the prosperous town.

As the volume of commercial traffic increased, the ability of the little creek to handle all the boats was stretched to the limit. It became clear that for the port of Petaluma to thrive the waterway would need periodic dredging to maintain an adequate navigable channel and turning basin. Federal laws empowered the U.S. Army Corps of Engineers to dredge channels for commercial ports along waterways, but only if they were on navigable rivers. In the years that followed the political clout of the Petaluma agri-industrial leaders was then brought to bear on the U.S. Congress. Little Petaluma Creek was officially declared a "river," and the Corps of Engineers began dredging.

For decades these actions allowed the river town to flourish. But after World War II, as commerce by road along a new highway network began to replace shipping on San Francisco Bay, the town began to turn its back on its downtown waterfront. As people then began to perceive of the river as a dirty, smelly drainage channel of little value, they allowed the wharves and buildings there to deteriorate. Across the country, many cities and towns were undergoing a similar transition, fencing off previously vibrant waterfront areas and treating them as nuisances or neglected "back-of-house" service areas. And in so doing, they accelerated the pollution and degradation of the waterways. Meanwhile, agricultural lands were being rapidly converted to suburbs, with development encroaching widely into floodplains. Fortunately, Petaluma acted to protect nearby agricultural lands by establishing the first-ever urban growth boundary in the country. But the action was not taken until

In the heart of downtown, the riverfront promenade features restaurants, shops, open space, and river views. 2021. Jose Luis Aranda.

significant damage had already been done to the river. Development in its watershed led to increased flooding and degradation of the riverine habitats. The town had acted bravely, but developers simply leapfrogged over it to other cities. The town's economic fortunes were ebbing, and it needed to reverse the trend.

By the early 1990s, the town recognized that the key to its economic resurgence would involve an ecologically responsible reclamation of the river corridor including its downtown river frontage. The landscape of this place, defined by the river, was what had given the town its distinctive character in years past, and it was what knitted it to its larger ecological setting. Revitalization of the riverfront could be central to the town's revival, and its rejuvenation might help reestablish its relationship with the natural environment.

My office was selected through a competitive process to prepare a plan for the 6.5-mile, 800-acre river corridor through the center of Petaluma. The multidisciplinary area plan took six years to complete, including an extensive process of community and regulatory agency outreach, before finally being adopted by unanimous vote into the city's general plan in 1996. Known officially as the Petaluma River Access and Enhancement Plan, it established a long-range vision for the physical transformation of the river corridor as well as a framework of policies and regulations that would enable its implementation by public agencies and riverfront property owners. Its overall goal was to establish systemwide balance between the natural and built environments, resource protections and public access, and public/private responsibilities. And, specifically, it addressed the restoration and preservation of the riverfront's natural and cultural resources, created a continuous riverfront greenway with trails and parks, encouraged a

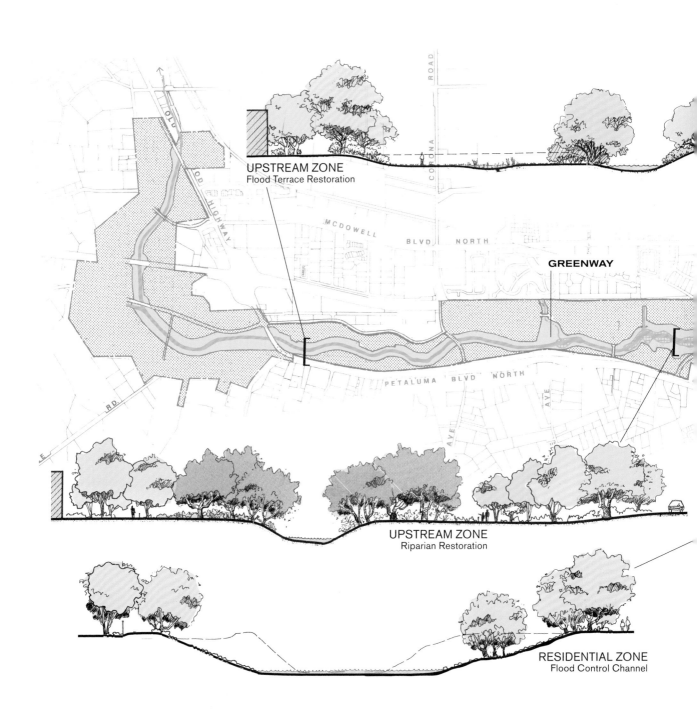

The River Plan guides developments along each segment of the 6.5 mile, 800-acre riverfront greenway revealing the core identity of the community. 1996. JNRA.

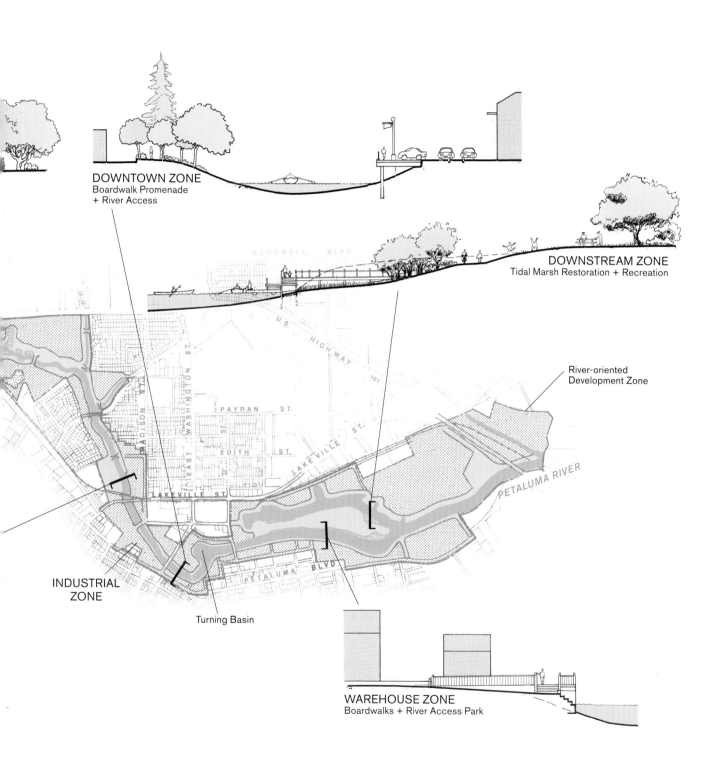

DOWNTOWN ZONE
Boardwalk Promenade
+ River Access

DOWNSTREAM ZONE
Tidal Marsh Restoration + Recreation

River-oriented
Development Zone

PETALUMA RIVER

**INDUSTRIAL
ZONE**

Turning Basin

WAREHOUSE ZONE
Boardwalks + River Access Park

A systemwide balance between the natural and built environments, resource protections and public access, and public/private responsibilities is established through the River Plan.

complementary balance of public and private uses along the river, and created the framework for a bustling commercial/recreational downtown waterfront as a joint public/private undertaking.

A key aspect of the plan was the creation of a 31.5-acre public riverfront park near the heart of downtown, which would include restored upland habitats, perimeter marsh restoration, recreational boat and kayak access, and a community education and recreation facility in a relocated historic barn. River-oriented industrial uses were retained, and a greenway and public trails were threaded through them to reveal the agri-industrial heritage of the town. Upstream, the plan also called for ecologically based flood management improvements to protect and enhance the remnant stands of riverine vegetation and heritage trees while expanding areas for flood protection and habitat restoration.

The natural spectrum of flowing water is now the defining feature of the town. And recognition of the importance of the entire riparian system — from fresh to salt water — now guides development within Petaluma for the benefit of the ecological system as well as urban and rural life. The protection and enhancement of that system is written into the fundamental regulatory framework controlling development along the corridor. And embedded in that approach is an understanding that thoughtful, well-conceived, and mutually supportive public activities along the corridor can coexist harmoniously with healthy nature. This marks a revolutionary change from the city's policies just a few years before. Today the city encourages private developments to comply with the plan and support a common vision of the importance of the public realm. Specific public projects have also been defined as catalysts. The scale of the undertaking allows a balance of human and natural uses to be integrated systemwide and at individual sites — a critical feature of landscape-scale change.

Since 1996 the plan has guided new developments, renovations, and ecological restorations along the entire river corridor. This has allowed the Petaluma riverfront to become one of the San Francisco Bay Area's most popular residential, tourist, and commercial destinations. New housing has also been built along each segment of the 6.5-mile corridor, bringing residents directly to the river's edge where they can enjoy riverfront

Left page: Access to the water is available throughout the greenway. 2021. Jose Luis Aranda.
Following page: The Turning Basin in the heart of downtown, normally a hub of river-oriented activity, is also a place of quiet connection to the river. 2021. Jose Luis Aranda.

It is the recognition of the importance of the entire riparian system – from fresh to salt water – that now guides all future developments within the town for the benefit of both the ecological system and urban life.

pathways and open spaces, recreational connections to the river, and restored riverfront vegetation. Meanwhile, in and around downtown at the center of the corridor, cafes, shops, offices, and mixed-use commercial developments have sprung up in new buildings and renovated warehouses overlooking the river. Plazas, parklets, promenades, and other pedestrian and bicycle connections have also been created along the river's greenway, linked to parallel shopping streets and a new SMART train station.

Through the planning and design process, serious differences among community members diminished as they discovered common goals and physical resolutions to seemingly intractable problems. By engaging in the creative process, they came to realize that they shared deeply held values about the landscape of their town. They found that they could work together through the process to protect those values, and that in doing so they could heal their community. As they developed a deeper understanding of the landscape of their town and clarified its importance to them as individuals and a community, they came together with a common vision of their town's future that has endured for more than two decades. ⊛

INTO SNOOPY'S HEAD

CHARLES M. SCHULZ MUSEUM AND RESEARCH CENTER
2301 Hardies Lane
Santa Rosa, CA

Right page: A garden promenade links the Museum with the campus and opens to the Snoopy Labyrinth on the left. 2021. JNRA.

In walking through the gardens and then writing about it, I realized how important it is for me to simply get lost in the sensual experience of a place.

A gravel path and richly textured garden lie beneath an allée of Chinese pistache trees between the Redwood Empire Skating Rink and the Charles M. Schulz Museum and Research Center in the Northern California town of Santa Rosa. Four parterres break out of the garden along the south side of the walk near the museum in an abstraction of a four-panel comic strip. And, as if reading between the lines, visitors can move between the garden panels to find another garden beyond. Here, the crushed stone paving leads to rushes and wild grasses at the edge of a wildflower meadow. And, beyond this, the paving and grasses arc together to form a curving pathway within the grassland, which twists and winds into a pattern that, seen from above, takes the shape of the head of one of Charles Schulz's most memorable characters: Charlie Brown's dog, Snoopy.

It is here, inside Snoopy's head, that a visitor can sit on a stone bench and gaze upon the setting for Snoopy's creation — the place made by Snoopy's creator and the building built to honor him. There are stones for sitting, located at the nose, the eye, the eyebrow, and near the center at the ear. Meanwhile, at the neck, just outside the entrance to the labyrinth, is a low stone seat wall, an abstraction of Snoopy's collar. Each of these sitting places is oriented in a slightly different direction, and each offers a slightly differing view of the complex across the labyrinth.

The idea for the labyrinth came to Jeannie Schulz, the wife of the famed Peanuts cartoonist, shortly after the terrorist attacks of September 11, 2001. She wanted to create a place in the common landscape for quiet personal reflection at that traumatic moment in U.S. history. Its form in the shape of Snoopy's head would tie a universal contemplative process to the memory of her beloved husband and his creations.

I was chosen to design the gardens and helped integrate the labyrinth into the site, for which Edwin Hamilton (who had worked with me on the Strybing Arboretum library terrace) did the stonework. When the labyrinth was mostly complete, I had a chance to walk it with Lea Goode-Harris, its designer, and she asked me to write about my experience of it for her. And in walking through the garden and writing about it, I realized how important it was to simply get lost in the sensual experience of a place. The places we create can affect us deeply and in unexpected ways. And if we are lucky, what we glean from the experience will endure, touching all that comes next. Sensual spatial experience is one of life's great pleasures and one of the best ways to learn about how places work.

This labyrinth is located outdoors and is part of a garden, but the pathway into Snoopy's head provokes an interior journey — a private experience in a public setting. Walking back and forth along a curving path, I was moving ever deeper into the grassland, never repeating the same steps, but reversing direction while continually approaching the center. Working through this landscape in such an intensively repetitive manner, stepping carefully, and observing similar but ever-changing vistas, a remarkable transformation began.

A labyrinth in the shape of Snoopy's head – the beloved Peanuts cartoon character - emerges from the grassland meadow at the entry to the museum. 2010. JNRA.

Individual blades of grass became more interesting than the sea of grass, as did individual pebbles in the gravel pathway. The physicality of the journey, the repetitive sequence, and the inward spiraling helped bring me to a meditative state.

By the time I reached the stone bench at Snoopy's ear, the goal at the end of the path, I had left the outside world behind. The journey was long enough, over 800 feet, and took enough time, that I had managed to leave the outside gracefully behind and enter a place inside the grasses and inside my own mind. I was not so much aware that I was inside Snoopy's head as that I was simply inside a special place. And from within this place, I could look across the space I had covered to the world outside and contemplate the setting that had nurtured Snoopy's creator. At the end of this interior journey I sensed at a personal level the essence of Charles Schulz's creativity, the force that had enabled him to develop the Peanuts comic strip and its beloved character, Snoopy. The journey was one that could move the traveler closer to a center. But the center we each find is our own.

I had not read the Peanuts strip for years. But since walking the labyrinth, I now find myself reading the old strips every day with renewed appreciation. They are far

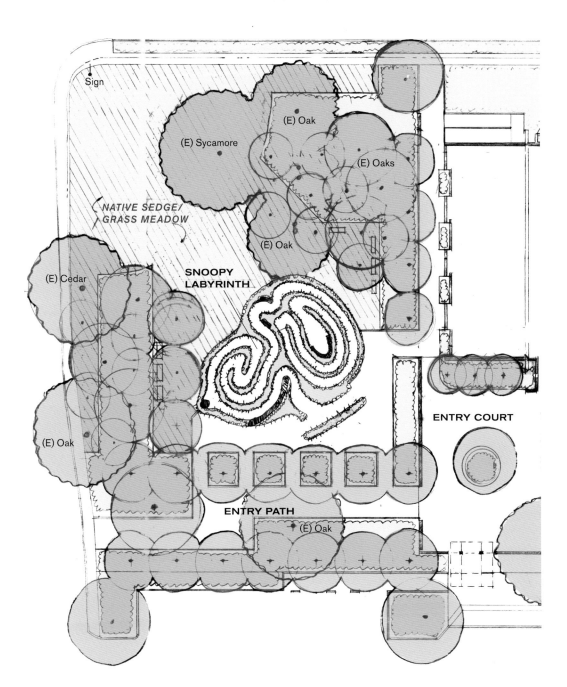

Sketch study showing Snoopy Labyrinth integrated into grassland meadow next to the garden allee. 2021. JNRA.

more interesting than I remembered. And I am much more aware of the introspective character of their gentle humor. The labyrinth experience — both the walking and the watching of the strangely focused behavior from the outside — seems to go to the heart of the Peanuts world.

The journey is one that moves the traveler closer to a center, and the center we each find is our own.

For me, however, the journey was not so much about Snoopy or Snoopy's creator as it was about my own connection to the landscape of that place. Totally immersed in its sights, sounds, and rhythms, I became detached from my ordinary life and was transported deeply into that landscape. This was not a wildland or a remote natural setting, but I found a similar spiritual connection to it as a place. I discovered the heart of this garden and the heart of this place that I had helped to create. And from the stone bench at its center, I could see relationships within the outdoor spaces and between those spaces and its surrounding buildings that I did not see before. There is a core to every place, and its discovery is a marvel.

The journey out of the labyrinth was along the same path that led me in. But I was walking with a new sense of the place. I was on the same path but seeing new things simply by looking in another direction. The curves of the pathway made me feel like I was on a joyful and endless journey with miles to go. I felt protected, even though I towered over the grasses. I was within a familiar place, but as in Alice's Wonderland, everything was somehow different. I had been deeply within this small place, and now my perceptions of it were changing in inexplicable ways. Much too quickly, I passed through the entrance and felt reborn.

This journey into Snoopy's head and out again was not what I had expected. I had expected a pleasant stroll along a garden path in a lovely setting. I didn't expect an inward journey of such intensity leading to such a heightened perception of the world around me. I also did not expect to learn so much about Charles Schulz and the world of Peanuts. A moment of quiet reflection while moving through that simple designed space revealed the power of the landscape to transform. ⊛

Left page: View across the entry gardens to the labyrinth and meadow. 2021. JNRA.

IDENTITY OF A
SMALL TOWN

YOUNTVILLE TOWN CENTER
6516 Washington Street at Yount Street
Yountville, CA

Right page: A public garden and gathering area was carved out of the former roadway as part of the new Town Center. 2018. Jose Luis Aranda.

Two critical considerations dictated the Community Center's location and created the Town Square – visibility of the Post Office entrance and accessibility for mobility-impaired people.

The small town of Yountville in the heart of the Napa Valley, just north of San Francisco, had for decades provided a home for agricultural workers at the valley's farms, vineyards, and wineries. A total of 1,600 in-town residents plus another 1,600 residents of the California Veterans Home combined to give it a total population of about 3,200. As a working-class community, it was largely passed over in the 1970s and 80s, as wine-related developments boomed up and down the valley and new residents flocked to more affluent towns such as Calistoga, Napa, and St. Helena. But eventually outsiders began to discover Yountville's small-town charm, lower real estate prices, and cheaper rents. And restaurateurs, resort owners, and second-home buyers soon began to turn their attention to the place, rapidly transforming it into a culinary center and premier resort destination. All the conflicts inherent in the transformation of a sleepy small-town to a world-renowned tourist destination were played out in the creation of its new town center.

As visitors began discovering Yountville, its longtime residents began to long for a common central place, one that would not be dedicated to the growing tourist economy. At that time there was no rural mail delivery service, and everyone had to visit the post office to pick up their mail. This made the post office an informal gathering space. Local residents had also built a barn-like community hall nearby where they held annual crab-feeds, community events, dances, and weddings. After a while, the townsfolk realized that the post office and community hall formed the basis of a town center, and that this could be made more attractive through the addition of other community-serving uses. In particular, a small public library might serve the needs of avid local readers, and a space for after-school and group activities was sorely needed. Building on this vision for a town center, my landscape architecture colleagues from UC Berkeley, Randy Hester and Marcia McNally, worked with the community over a period of two years to develop a conceptual master plan that would include these new uses and be located between the community hall and the post office.

After the master plan was approved by the city council Randy and Marcia arranged for the town to hire me to carry on this work. Personal relationships counted in such a place where everyone knew each other and had depended upon one another for generations. By a simple recommendation from a trusted colleague, I was immediately and warmly accepted into the community as one who would act in their best interests. And for the next ten years, followed by two more years of legal wrangling with the main contractor, the architect Susi Marzuola and I carried the project through to completion. The two of us worked closely with a locally appointed committee of residents, conducted community-wide workshops and design sessions, collaborated with staff, adjusted plans in response to changing political climates, helped residents understand the funding process, oversaw construction, and finally celebrated its completion with a memorable dinner at one of the outstanding restaurants that had by then been well integrated into the town. The project ended up earning national

The Town Square formed by the Community Hall, the Post Office, and the new Community Center is the center of the small town's public life. 2018. Jose Luis Aranda.

recognition for its environmental sustainability, ecologically based design, and steadfast reflection of local community values in changing times.

Over the long period of planning and design, the community changed dramatically. A community of working families who tended and picked the crops in nearby fields, repaired machinery, shopped in local markets, and made wine from grapes they had grown came

increasingly to reflect the values of more affluent, ex-urban society. Many new residents were interested in small-town rural life. But others were disconnected from the soil — more interested in drinking fine wines rather than making them, in dining in fine restaurants rather than attending community clam bakes. The conversations about the new town center changed with this new mix of residents.

There in the parking lot was a covey of quail, young and old happily feeding on the plants in one area and scurrying across to the cover in another, clucking boisterously. The parking lot had become a wildlife sanctuary.

Our central charge was to site and design a new community center building on gently sloping land between the existing community hall and the post office. Plans called for it to be a high-ceilinged, single-story building with a multipurpose space sized for full court basketball, a library, an art room, a teen room, offices, bathrooms, lockers, and storage. Two critical considerations dictated the community center's location and created the town square: visibility of the post office entrance and accessibility for mobility-impaired people.

First and foremost, the new building could not block the view between the existing community hall and post office. The residents had to be able to see who was coming and going at the post office. This moved the new building back from the Washington Street frontage. The resultant open space, however, could be treated as a town square, right on the main street of town, formed and activated by the three buildings that faced it. Meanwhile, to the rear of the building, a parking lot was required for users of the town center and for workers in the various restaurants and businesses that were then emerging in the downtown area. And beneath the parking lot was a geothermal field that would serve the building's ground-source heating and cooling systems. The size of the parking lot with its underground heat pump system thus determined the back limit of the building.

The second principal consideration was that the entire complex had to be wholly accessible to people with disabilities. And since approximately half the residents of the town were disabled veterans living in the Veterans Home, it was important to exceed minimum code requirements. This consideration set the floor level for the new building at a height that would allow access on all four sides and between the neighboring buildings. If the front of the new building was thus to flow directly onto the town square, the plaza would need to be at a level several feet below that of the sidewalk on Washington Street. However, this created an ideal condition for an amphitheater-like design that might separate the square from the commercial uses along Washington Street. It would also allow the square to be at the same level as the post office and its visitor parking, making the entire complex wholly accessible. The grading required to get all these pieces to fit together seamlessly (and seemingly without effort) was a tour-de-force of technical and spatial design.

Facing due west and south, deep overhangs integrated into the buildings would provide shaded relief around the edges of the plaza in the heat of the summer, but additional cooling of the plaza itself would be a benefit. The town manager, a fourth-generation Yountvillian whose family had a long history of agricultural work, suggested that we create a fountain based on the winemaking process that would both honor the heritage of the community and create an opportunity to repurpose interesting grape-processing equipment that the old-timers knew well. With this idea in mind, we designed an interactive, cascading fountain that kids could operate by adapting common equipment to control the flow of water in an abstraction of the winemaking process. The longtime residents and young family members on the committee were thrilled with the proposal and identified it with the pleasure and work of their place.

A symbol of identity for the local community and welcoming to new and old residents alike.

However, by this time in the process, the city council had changed, and none of the new members were interested in either the playful interactive aspect of a fountain or the reference to the industrial production process. They explicitly stated that it did not reflect the new sophisticated image of the town they wanted to project. Encouraged by the new members, they instead promoted a fountain design that mimicked the elegant expensive styles of nearby resorts. This revealed a subtle shift in priorities and conflicts within the changing community. The leaders were beginning to treat the town square as a showplace for visitors, not a place for locals to congregate. In the end, because of cost, no fountain was included. Cooling would instead have to come from portable umbrellas. The underlying conflicts would also resurface near the end of the process.

Another important feature of the project derived from the fact that downtown Yountville is located very near a tributary stream that flows to the Napa River. Indeed, the proposed town center parking lot lay partially within this stream's floodplain. This ecological association provided a cue for the overall landscape design for the project: we could re-create an ecological continuum in this densely developed urban environment through generous

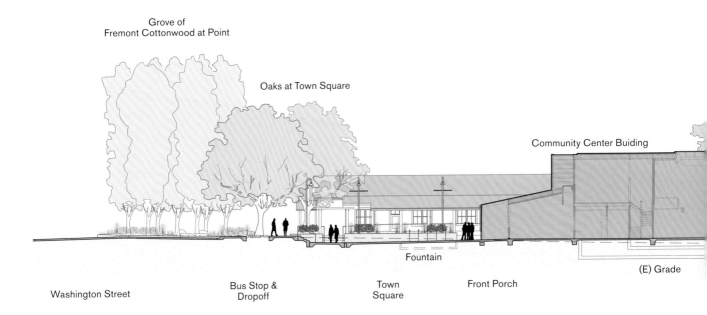

Grove of
Fremont Cottonwood at Point

Oaks at Town Square

Community Center Buiding

Fountain

(E) Grade

Washington Street

Bus Stop &
Dropoff

Town
Square

Front Porch

Cross section through Town Square and Community Center from Washington Street to parking lot showing
sub-surface stormwater capture and ground source heat pump systems. 2008. JNRA.

planting, a stormwater capture system, and composed wildlife linkages. All stormwater
would thus be collected on site, treated in constructed bioswales to filter and control the
runoff, and be allowed to recharge into the ground, with the excess discharged to the creek
in surface channels. As part of this system, the parking lot, lying closest to the creek in the
floodplain, would be designed to handle periodic flooding while collecting and distributing
the overall site's rainwater. It would also be planted as a native sycamore grove with riparian
understory vegetation in the spaces between the cars, enabling significant habitat value to be
created out of an ordinary parking lot. The town square and other public-use areas on higher
ground would meanwhile be treated as upland habitat with oak groves, grasses, perennials,
and other native plant species typically found in the upper parts of the valley, and with the
square itself treated as an urban oak savannah.

I was convinced that through careful selection and placement of vegetation our
design could create significant new wildlife habitat within the urban core, but I wasn't
prepared for what I encountered on my first visit after the project was complete. There in
the parking lot was a covey of quail, young and old birds happily feeding on the plants in
one area and scurrying across to the cover provided by another, clucking boisterously. The
parking lot had become a wildlife sanctuary. I also looked up into the trees we had planted
and discovered flocks of birds flying between the creek and the town center. Urban ecology
was working.

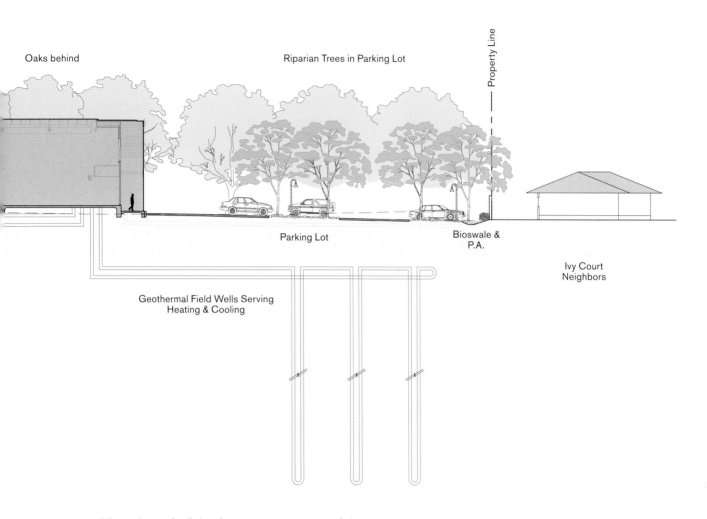

Oaks behind

Riparian Trees in Parking Lot

Property Line

Parking Lot

Bioswale & P.A.

Ivy Court Neighbors

Geothermal Field Wells Serving Heating & Cooling

Near the end of the design process, one of the most active and creative members of the citizen committee, a longtime resident, announced that she could no longer support the project. She felt it was an ostentatious display of wealth and too out of character with the working heritage of the town. She placed an initiative on the ballot opposing the project, bringing issues of local gentrification and change to the fore. The initiative was defeated, and the town proceeded with the project, paid for by an increased tax on the resorts and tourists. But new and old residents found themselves at odds with each other, and the comradery and common purpose that had blossomed through the design process was shaken. However, the vote ultimately confirmed that our plans truly reflected the interests, needs, and aspirations of a new, blended community. The town was changing; adaptation was difficult, but a new identity was being forged built respectfully upon the old.

Following page: Shaded overhangs surrounding the Town Square with seating and artwork attract a steady stream of locals and visitors alike. 2018. Jose Luis Aranda.

Despite the rough spots, the project was a resounding success. It establishes a true center for this small town as a symbol of identity for the local community. It is welcoming to new and old residents alike. Outsiders see the fancy restaurants and resorts as defining features of Yountville, but the locals see it differently. This is their place. The town center, however, reflects the values and aspirations of both a vanishing generation and the new ones who are now calling this place home. It is a beautiful, simple, modest but elegant public space that fits comfortably with the native landscape and incorporates the best of current environmentally sustainable technologies. Conceived as a flexible armature for future adaptations, it now houses several outdoor sculptures integral to the Yountville Art Walk. It is the centerpiece of the public commons — a source of enduring community pride and identity of place. ✳

Left page: Community Center, Town Square, and public gardens seen from Washington Street. 2018. Jose Luis Aranda.

WINE AND FRIENDSHIP

STAG'S LEAP WINE CELLARS
5766 Silverado Trail
Napa, CA

Right page: Perched dramatically at the edge of a plateau, the visitor center overlooks the hidden valley's creek, vineyards, and volcanic mountains. 2021. JNRA.

Like the waves from a pebble tossed
into a pond, the human connections of
places are ever-expanding circles, often
with rich and unforeseen ramifications.

T he phone call from a stranger saying that Betsy Rogers had given me an outstanding reference threw me for a loop. I had never heard of Betsy Rogers. The caller was inviting me to a meeting at a prestigious winery in the Napa Valley where I would be allowed to present my landscape architecture credentials. Convinced that this was a crank call, I made my first-ever Google search. I thought that perhaps I could find out who the person was who had recommended me, but with my limited media/tech skills, I found no useful references. Nonetheless, I was intrigued and was able to confirm that the Stag's Leap Wine Cellars was legitimate. I was sure that they had contacted me by mistake, but a door had been opened, and I would step through it.

My work until this time had been mostly with public agencies, focused on community building and redefining our culture's relationship with the natural environment. But, after the interview, I was offered the commission to help the winery owner, Warren Winiarski, design a new visitor center in collaboration with his architect from Barcelona, Spain. At first I was uncomfortable with the commercial aspect of the project, but I liked the relationship the owner had established between his winery and the natural setting. I also liked his description of the creative process of transforming grapes into wine. Yes, this was a commercial enterprise, but it was one that was agriculturally based, grounded in a land ethic, and linked inextricably with environmental stewardship. The intertwined ecological, agricultural, educational, aesthetic, and human aspects of this place appeared consistent with the public work I had been doing. I accepted the commission.

Still thinking that the referral was a mistake, without revealing my ignorance to the client, I continued to explore other avenues to find out who had recommended me. Thus it was that months later I discovered that Warren had asked a colleague of his at New York City's Central Park Conservancy for a recommendation for his project. That colleague had immediately contacted a friend of hers at UC Berkeley's College of Environmental Design. Her friend had been unable to help but had referred her to another faculty member, an old friend of mine, who had in fact recommended me. That friend, Louise Mozingo, knew me as an educator who was committed to creative, ecologically based community design and who had created beautiful outdoor spaces. The original call I had received had not been a mistake after all. Moreover, this revelation about the process of referral prompted me to reflect on the network of relationships that sustain us and that lie beneath the conception of places.

We create places for and with people. These are human actions taken by a collection of people for the purpose of serving human needs at a particular place and time. Scientists, engineers, architects, owners, regulators, and affected communities are all collaborators in the creative act of placemaking. But so are the people who make the referrals and those who use the place once it is constructed. Although mostly unseen in the final physical form, this web of human interactions is central to the identity of a place and to all who touch and are touched by it. Like the waves from a pebble tossed into a pond,

The form of the Visitor Center building was derived from the rugged volcanic setting. 2021. JNRA.

human connections to a place may take the form of an ever-expanding circle. And, as in this case, it may be rich with unforeseen ramifications.

Warren had built his winery from a small family operation into a large commercial facility that produced some of the best wines in the world — all the while maintaining a strong sense of environmental stewardship that included paying intense attention to every aspect of the growing and winemaking process. The family, however, was now interested in transforming the winery's visitor experience to make it worthy of their world-class wines. This meant moving the visitor areas out of a funky old processing barn into a new building somewhere within the grounds. Warren's initial preference had been to adapt an area in the center of winemaking operation so that visitors could experience the complex and magical process he treasured. But his family's preference, and that of the Spanish architect, was to create a tasting and sales area in a more remote site, one that overlooked the vineyards and a

hidden valley at the back of the property. My first role was to produce site designs for these two areas to help determine which would be the preferred location for the new building and a corresponding identity of place.

To kick off the design work, Warren convened a meeting of the design team's architect, engineers, landscape architect, and staff. But his primary purpose was to introduce the Spanish architect to me to ensure that we would be able to work together. The two of us met as coffee was brought in, and began a cordial conversation, each looking for common ground. As a high school student, the first people my brother and I had met when my family moved to California had been three Spanish sisters from Barcelona. They had moved to the area with their family the exact same day we did, and we had become close friends. Over the next two years, we had discovered California together, supporting each other as we moved into young adulthood. But we had not been in contact for more than

A reunion with the Valls Klein family in Spain after 50 years, the culmination of connections made through the Stag's Leap Wine Cellars project. 2011. Elena Vasquez Valls.

forty years. Talking to the Barcelona architect, Javier Barba, however, it occurred to me they might have run in the same circles as him in Spain, so I asked him if he knew them. To my great delight, he replied that he did know them well. And after that Javier and I talked excitedly for half an hour about our mutual acquaintances. Warren watched as a new friendship blossomed at his winery.

In the weeks that followed that initial meeting I prepared two detailed alternative site plans for the new visitor center derived from both the overall winery operation and its landscape setting: one a building integrated within the industrial complex of the winery, and another knitted into the natural/agrarian landscape. Each option required rethinking the relationship between the production and visitor facilities, so as to accommodate new pulses of visitors while maintaining the efficiency of the winemaking operations. Each also reconceived the visitor arrival experience, parking, circulation, gathering areas, and the overall character of the built environment. In the end, Warren was satisfied I had given his preference a fair treatment, but the weight of opinion favored the more remote site, and this was the one that was selected.

In the chosen scheme the building would become a primary destination, featuring distinctive architecture with rich details and providing gracious accommodations for visitors. But in contrast to other wineries then being built throughout the Napa Valley, the site plan placed the building at the edge of a dramatic space, not at its center. The new place created by the building and its associated site developments would thus focus attention on the agrarian and natural landscapes that support the extraordinary grapes grown at this location. Warren, his family, and the design team all agreed that the building should be an important supporting part of this landscape, not its main feature.

The hillside plateau chosen for the new building was at the same level as the core of the winery's industrial operations and storage caves. But it was also removed from it so that it looked eastward over vineyards, the creek, the hidden valley, and the dramatic Stag's Leap rock outcropping on the ridgeline above. It is a breathtakingly beautiful site. To reach it, we decided to create a new public entrance from Silverado Trail, the road on which the winery is located on the east side of Napa Valley. From here a new entry drive would create a new sequence of arrival that gradually unveiled the complex layering of the landscape, bypassing the processing buildings to reveal the vineyards and landscape to their rear. The entry drive terminated near the creek, where visitors were offered a dramatic view of the vineyards within the hidden valley ringed by volcanic mountains, with the new visitor building in the distance. Fire and water had created this place, combining over time to make the unique soils in which the grapes thrive. And it is this volcanic soil that is featured in the first display in the visitor center — even before the award-winning wines.

From the end of the drive, visitors would walk to the new building along a curving garden path rising above the vineyards and the creek, where they were provided with views of the whole landscape. The building itself was designed as an iconic, sculpted form derived from the rugged geology. A stone-faced pavilion set against the oak-wooded hillside and perched above the valley, its indoor and outdoor spaces flowed together effortlessly as an integral part and extension of its beautiful setting. It offered a series of spaces where people could collect to take in the scenery while enjoying each other's company and the bounty of the place. The built environment thus respectfully balanced ecological, agricultural, industrial, and human uses. Of course, on arrival, most visitors will be more interested in the wine than in the placemaking. It is a place that can nurture friendships over a glass of wine. But their experience of it will be greatly enhanced by its being set within a carefully designed landscape that carries lessons about ecological stewardship, agricultural sustainability, creativity, and the identity of place.

As the design process was reaching its initial conclusion, our daughter, Taya, announced that she would be getting married that summer. I asked Warren if he would be amenable to trading my time as a design professional for his wine for the wedding. My hourly rate at the time was the same as the price of a bottle of his wine. He was delighted with the idea, and so we exchanged our services in the way of past generations — and in so doing formed a different bond. This was not a commercial transaction but an act of friendship and mutual respect. After her marriage, Taya and her new husband then took their honeymoon in Spain, and Javier showed them around Barcelona. The place that I had

Following page: The Visitor Center emerges from the oak woodlands on the hillside, overlooking the valley landscape, vineyards, and the Stag's Leap palisade. 2021. JNRA.

The building and its associated site developments would focus attention on the agrarian and natural landscapes. Fire and water created this place, combining over time to make the unique volcanic soils in which the grapes thrive.

designed, the people with whom I had collaborated, and the product of that land would help launch our daughter into her new life.

Javier also gave me the cell phone number in Spain of my dear old friend (and my date for our high school junior prom) Babette Valls Klein. I called her one day out of the blue, and the surprise nearly caused her to have an accident while driving along a mountain road. We then began to communicate and discovered an enduring friendship contained within our old memories. Eventually, Jody and I travelled to Spain, and we reunited with the family as grandparents sharing the warmth, welcome, and experiences of a lifetime. My community-based placemaking had expanded my web of personal and professional relationships while serendipitously bringing together long-lost friends who had never forgotten each other. The place of fire and water, magical transformation of grapes to wine, and harmoniously balanced wild and cultivated nature is also, for me, a place that nurtured human connection, enriched friendships, and supported creative partnerships. ⊛

HOMETOWN COMMUNITY-BUILDING

ARTS AS CATALYST
Addison Street Arts District

GARDENS IN THE CENTER OF THE CITY
Berkeley Central Library and Library Gardens/K Street Flats

STREET THEATER
Fourth Street Paseo

ALMOST CLEAN AND GREEN
North Waterfront Park & Cesar Chavez Memorial Solar Calendar

Berkeley

HOMETOWN
COMMUNITY-BUILDING

Berkeley is the place that Jody and I have chosen to call home for more than fifty years. This place, with its diverse people, rich cultural heritage, and natural environment, has nurtured us, just as it once nurtured a Native American and Spanish/Mexican population before the founding of the present-day city in the mid-1800s. Like many other residents of Berkeley who each in their own way have actively contributed to the common well-being of their city, it has been important for us to not just take what is offered from the past or depend solely upon others to chart a course for the future. We have rather sought to engage creatively with our community to make a difference. This was one of the great lessons learned from the rebuilding of society that followed the social, economic, environmental, and racial upheavals of the 1960s-1970s. Progress could not just be the work of paid professionals and politicians. More often than not, it was ordinary citizens committed to the well-being of their community who brought about meaningful change.

When we first moved to Berkeley, the physical environment of the city was deteriorating rapidly. Fear, isolation, and neglect had taken their toll following the antiwar, free-speech, and racial protests of the late 1960s and 1970s. Shuttered and fortress-like

Sketch of Fran Violich and John Roberts at Berkeley City Council
meeting. 1986. Evany Zirul.

buildings that turned their backs on the streets were being built; there was deep distrust of
the public sector and its institutions; and derelict public spaces supported hostile, aggressive
street behavior and disrespect for the built environment. These adverse conditions affected
us directly as a family, and I became motivated to be part of the repair of our city. What I
could contribute was expertise in the design of the physical environment. Over the past fifty
years, I have thus been directly involved, either as a volunteer designer, hired professional,
or consultant oversight manager in more than fifty projects for public agencies and private
property owners interested in improvements to the public realm.

  With the encouragement of my old mentor from UC Berkeley, Francis Violich,
I joined several different groups of architects, landscape architects, planners, merchants,
interested citizens, and property owners to articulate new visions for the public realm
and work for their implementation. This was mostly placemaking through enlightened
grassroots community activism, guided by seasoned professionals, and supported by city
officials, property owners, and merchants. In common cause, people were coming together
to reimagine a better place, to pressure the authorities to make substantive changes for
community benefit, and to convince the citizens to vote to fund improvements. Envisioning

changes to the physical environment had become a key community-building tool and a newfound source of pride in our place.

With one notable exception, my work in Berkeley has involved community-based urban design, in contrast to the more ecologically based work I have done for public resource agencies. Its focus has been on the character, quality, and inclusiveness of the city's outdoor environments as a forum for daily public life. As part of this effort, however, I have consistently sought to bring nature into the city, either by making substantive changes to the urban fabric or by simply adding trees. The exception was a radical plan to reclaim the Berkeley landfill in an experimental attempt at ecological restoration.

Common to all the projects in Berkeley has been the planting of trees. This simple but profoundly important action benefits the community and the immediate urban environment while also helping to address such critical issues as poor air quality, heat island effects, carbon sequestration, and global warming. Most of the city is today a designed landscape: a former grassland that has largely been converted into a diverse urban forest, which thrives in a generally benign climate as a consequence of year-round watering. Trees bring nature into the built environment, providing habitat for birds, urban wildlife, and insects. They give human scale to the architecture and infrastructure while enriching the outdoor spaces with sculptural shapes, shade, color, fragrance, texture, and sound. And trees in the public right-of-way, in combination with those on private property, combine to create a landscape in a largely built environment with many of the attributes of a wildland forest.

Berkeley's trees are an eclectic mix of native and exotic species originating from the four corners of the earth, much like the eclectic mix of people who live there. And the distinctive character of different areas throughout the city is due in large part to the trees. I have been directly responsible for the planting of more than 2,000 trees within the city of Berkeley. Among these are the revived oak woodlands and restored riparian forests along Blackberry Creek in North Berkeley, which have rejuvenated a wildlife corridor between the hills and San Francisco Bay. They include the European hornbeams that frame the entry to the Addison Street Arts District — which combine with London plane, red maple, and hackberry trees to give downtown Berkeley a lush and orderly natural character. Elsewhere, towering Lombardy poplars mark the edge of the Bayer Pharmaceuticals campus and the beginning of the West Berkeley Artisan District; a stately cork oak graces the courtyard of the West Berkeley Branch Library as part of a regional "re-oaking" of California; and spring-flowering Akebono cherry trees will one day create a joyous welcome for visitors to the North Berkeley Senior Center.

The stories that follow describe some of the small and big ways I have helped to change the commons of my home community. ⊙

Left page: Akebono Cherry trees now grace the North Berkely Senior Center. 2021. JNRA.

ARTS AS CATALYST

ADDISON STREET ARTS DISTRICT
Addison Street, between Shattuck Ave. and Milvia Street
Berkeley, CA

Right page: Berkeley Repertory Theater courtyard between the Roda and Peet's theaters anchors the Addison Street Arts District. 2018. Jose Luis Aranda.

The arts and cultural venues were the real economic engine and would become the focus of the City's revitalization efforts.

Once a hub of activity and a vibrant commercial center, by the early 1980s downtown Berkeley had become creepy, dirty, and hostile — a place of vacant storefronts, few residents, an increasingly violent drug culture, and a generally neglected physical environment. Few people felt comfortable enough to spend much time there, and a serious revitalization was needed. But how could the city best focus its efforts to transform this place and generate positive activity?

After some difficult soul searching, city leaders concluded that arts and cultural activities were what compelled people to come downtown. Shopping was no longer a principal attraction, but irrespective of dirt and disorder, people would still come for the theater, movies, and related cultural activities. Venues for art and culture were the real economic engine on which the city should focus its revitalization efforts.

So far, this economic analysis has proven correct. The arts have indeed become a catalyst for the broader economic revitalization of the downtown area, and they have brought spin-off developments like restaurants, bookstores, galleries, and related activities. People now live downtown, too, something never foreseen or encouraged by earlier city ordinances or bank lending policies. But this cultural renaissance would require institutional changes to create basic incentives for investors as well as renewed commitment by the community to embrace a new vision of the place.

A first step toward this vision came when the mayor and city staff were able to convince the Berkeley Repertory Theater not to move to Oakland. Then, when the city facilitated the purchase of properties for the theater company's expansion on Addison Street, Berkeley Rep became the anchor for a newly declared Addison Street Arts District. With committed property owners, a renowned arts venue, a supportive city staff, and a city council anxious to strategically invest public funds, the key elements for a revitalization of place seemed to be falling into place.

Next, a small group of Addison Street property owners (including Berkeley Rep), the city's economic development staff, an architect, and I, got together to figure out what an Addison Street Arts District could be, how its physical form might be conceived, and what it would take for it to flourish. I prepared an urban-design plan showing how to retrofit the street with widened sidewalks, trees, pedestrian lighting, entry markers, and integrated artwork. Zoning changes would also be instituted to encourage arts-related uses within the buildings. Indeed, art would become integral to the basic structure of the space, signaling that creativity in all its forms could flourish here. As we conceived it, the transformation of Addison Street would take place in phases over several years, beginning with basic engineering changes to create more gracious pedestrian experience, narrow the space for vehicles, and slow the traffic down. The block would be treated as an elongated plaza, designed to accommodate festivals, outdoor concerts, and theatrical events. And the sidewalks themselves would become venues for art — in the paving, on the walls, at entryways, and as free-standing expressions.

I was especially interested in the incorporation of words and language arts into the fabric of the space. I thought we could embed poetry, but wasn't sure how to do it. Impulsively, one evening, as the concrete curbs were being poured during an early round of improvements, Jody and I tried to inscribe stanzas from The Rubaiyat by Omar Khayyam into them using old letterpress printing tools. Our guerrilla act was singularly unsuccessful — although the concrete was still wet, it set up too quickly, and the lettering was virtually illegible. But the idea of wrapping the entire block in poetry remained compelling.

Susie Medak, the executive director of Berkeley Rep, shared my enthusiasm for poetry in the street. She convinced Robert Hass, a former U.S. poet laureate, professor, and Berkeley resident, to select poems to be inscribed there. Hass and his assistant, Jessica Fisher, chose short poems from a wide assortment of works connected in some way to Berkeley, and with subject matter related to the activities of the buildings along the street. Ohlone songs translated by early Berkeley faculty; poems of early Californio settlers; Beat Era poems; poems by Nobel Prize winners, Pulitzer Prize winners, and poets laureate; compelling verses from songwriters, playwrights, activists, and ordinary people — all would be included. The poems were embossed on 127, 2'x2' cast-iron tiles designed by local artists and set into the sidewalk in roughly chronological order in a regular rhythm up and down the street. At the celebration of the poetry installation, the assembled poets joined together to sing "Puff the Magic Dragon," as the author, a Berkeley guy, read it aloud.

The collection reflects the cultural heritage of the city through poetry, and it provides a glimpse of the rich literary role Berkeley has played in the country. People walking down the sidewalk now bump into others who have stopped to read the embedded stanzas, and conversations follow. The Berkeley Poetry Walk was immediately recognized as a National Landmark by the American Poetry Association, and its contents were published as The Addison Street Anthology by the local Heyday Press. A poem of mine, "One," about being born a twin, was included in the collection. Bob Hass wanted the voice of the designer of the arts district to be included. I was beaming as it was inscribed into the sidewalk.

Added to the mix of poetry on the sidewalk are twelve paving-art pieces by local artists selected by the Civic Arts Commission. One artist set an abstract sea of sculpted lips and a few pairs of ears into the paving. Her intention had been to suggest that more people talked than listened in Berkeley. But once her work was installed and she saw someone walk across the lips, she declared that people's feet would now be kissed as they walked down the sidewalk. This was a radically different and more intimate perception of downtown than that of just a few years before. But both messages were true. What had started as an idea among a small group of people had now blossomed into a community-wide effort.

Berkeley Repertory Theater, the original anchor for the arts district, was soon joined by other small theaters as well as other arts groups wanting to create venues on the block. These initially included the JazzSchool, with its performance space and small

The Berkeley Poetry Walk was immediately recognized by the American Poetry Association as a National Poetry Landmark and subsequently published as *The Addison Street Anthology* by the local Heyday Press.

restaurant; Freight & Salvage, a renowned old-time and bluegrass music club; theater training facilities; the Aurora Theater, a small theater company; Capoeira, a Brazilian dance school and performance space; and a curated art gallery/exhibition space that occupies the ground floor frontage of a city parking structure. As the various venues fed off each other, the synergy began to create a vibrant district, humming with activity, which brings people and energy from the wider Bay Area to downtown Berkeley.

Community-design efforts are typically implemented incrementally as funding is secured, resulting in a somewhat eclectic, organic pattern of implementation. In this case, the sorely needed pedestrian lighting has been postponed, awaiting sufficient public clamor to make it a city budget priority. Similarly, the transformation of the street right-of-way itself into a pedestrian zone that allows cars (rather than a roadway that allows pedestrians) has yet to happen. But as the district evolves and more people come to understand the value of a shift in urban culture from a focus on cars to a focus on people, the appropriate physical and policy changes may yet come to pass.

Meanwhile, hoped-for spin-off developments from the arts district have been far greater than anyone imagined. New housing is now being developed for people to live downtown. Restaurants and bookstores are flourishing. UC Berkeley's Art Museum and Pacific Film Archive has relocated from a site south of the university to a downtown site, extending the arts district across Shattuck Avenue to the west edge of the campus. The Jewish Museum, the David Brower Center, a new hotel/conference center, and other arts and cultural institutions have likewise found new homes in the vicinity. A new civic identity and pride of place is emerging from the Addison Street Arts District — a creative idea that is giving a new sense of place to downtown Berkeley. ⊛

Following page: Addison Street with widened sidewalk, poetry panels, and embedded artwork. 2016. Hanh Nguyen.

GARDENS IN THE CENTER OF THE CITY

BERKELEY CENTRAL LIBRARY AND LIBRARY GARDENS/K STREET FLATS
2020 Kittredge Street,
Berkeley, CA

Right page: Gardens of a semi-public plaza create an oasis in the heart of downtown. 2016. Hanh Nguyen.

Remarkably, at the time, there were very few places for outdoor seating or open plazas for public use in downtown Berkeley.

B erkeley's Central Library is a treasured Art Deco building, listed on the National Register of Historic Places as one of the country's most significant historic architectural resources. It is also one of many beautiful historic buildings that grace a nationally recognized downtown historic district. And it happens to be the most heavily visited building in downtown Berkeley.

In the early 2000s, the citizens of Berkeley elected to double its size. The architects proposed a respectful modern addition extending to an adjacent lot but set back from the corner of the old building along Kittredge Street to highlight its handsome historic facade. Accessibility was a key consideration in this project which also included renovation of the old building. In a creative leap, the architects proposed that a new main entry, which would connect through a glazed atrium to the new building, be carved out of the basement level of the old building to meet modern standards. The setback from Kittredge Street would provide sufficient space to create a small plaza descending to this new combined entry. It would provide room for an accessible ramp in combination with a grand stair, seating, trees, plantings, and bicycle parking. Remarkably, at the time there were very few places for outdoor seating or open plazas for public use in downtown Berkeley. In fact, they had been actively discouraged by the city since the turmoil of the 1960s. But the little plaza we designed in front of the new entry was greeted with enthusiasm. Indeed, it helped begin a process of making a more people-friendly public realm downtown, one that would encourage, rather than discourage, community gatherings.

The property immediately next door to the library, at the terminus of a one-block-long side street, contained a multistory parking garage that had formerly served the once-popular Hink's Department Store nearby. The structure covered the entire lot, butting up directly against the wall of the new library addition. But after the library expansion was complete, its adjacent property's developer, John DeClercq, initiated a planning and design process to build a five-story apartment building, ground-floor retail space, and sub-surface parking there. I was hired to work with the architect to help design outdoor spaces for this new building complex that would complement the library and its new entry plaza. Our response was to extend the library plaza and use the landscaped open space as a transition between the two structures. The new building would be set apart from the library by sixty feet, creating a visual extension of the right-of-way of the short tree-lined street that terminated there. The resulting open space combined with the library's entry plaza creates a garden in the heart of downtown. We imagined this both as usable open space for the residential and corner commercial tenants in the new building as well as a visual amenity from within the library.

As configured, this open space has since become a model for other such spaces downtown. Its most prominent feature is a water wall/sculpture that aligns with the library's new entry wing and forms a lively backdrop for a small semi-public plaza. This presently

Historic Building
BERKELEY CENTRAL LIBRARY   Library Main Entry

Elevation along Kittredge Street showing Berkeley Central Library and library addition, gardens, and apartment complex. 2002. JNRA.

contains sunny outdoor seating for a corner restaurant on the ground floor of the new apartment complex. But the water wall/sculpture also separates this publicly accessible front garden/plaza, which has become one of the most popular spots in downtown Berkeley, from a private rear garden for residents of the apartment complex. The incorporation of artwork here was, of course, consistent with the emerging arts and cultural identity for downtown. But in combination with trees around the plaza, it also creates an artful landscape terminus to a short side street that once ended in a multistoried parking structure.

An additional and unusual gift to the community was embedded in the siting of the apartment blocks and open spaces on the podium level of the new building, which is now known as the K Street Flats. These were assembled so as to frame an open view toward San Francisco Bay from the west-facing windows of a new children's reading room. The original charter for the library stated that children reading Robert Louis Stevenson's Treasure Island in the reading room should always be able to look out its window to see San Francisco Bay's own Treasure Island. The configuration of the five towers and courtyards on the podium was designed in direct response to this aspect of the charter.

The new public and private spaces of the Central Berkeley Library, its entry plaza, and the adjacent library gardens complement each other and together create an unusual and well-used oasis. Moreover, the termination of a once derelict and unsightly side street now provides a soothing urban landscape destination just off the city's main commercial

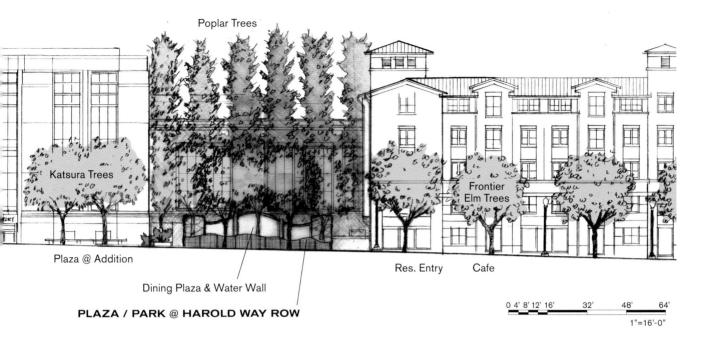

Poplar Trees

Katsura Trees

Frontier
Elm Trees

Plaza @ Addition

Res. Entry   Cafe

Dining Plaza & Water Wall

PLAZA / PARK @ HAROLD WAY ROW

0 4' 8' 12' 16'   32'   48'   64'

1"=16'-0"

The public and private spaces
complement each other and, together,
create an unusual and well-used
oasis in the center of town – a whole
experience that is greater than the
individual parts.

boulevard. These spaces reflect a profound change toward a more welcoming, comfortable, and well-tended public realm. Incrementally, each such addition contributes to a whole experience that is greater than the individual parts. It is hard to imagine that such places were once discouraged in downtown Berkeley. I love bringing visitors to this place, and I hope it will be here for many years. ⊛

Following page: A kinetic water wall forms the colorful backdrop to the plaza and provides privacy to the private gardens. 2016. Hanh Nguyen.

STREET
THEATER

FOURTH STREET PASEO
Between 4th and 5th Streets, south of Hearst
Berkeley, CA

Right page: The Paseo creates a lively mid-block passageway between the neighborhood and the shopping district. 2018. Jose Luis Aranda.

The stage set, with entries and exits, textured pavement, interconnected rooms, festive lighting, greenery, and spaces for musicians was composed for people to strut their stuff…

The developer of the Fourth Street retail district in west Berkeley, Denny Abrams, has long been known for creative consideration of the public realm. And since the beginning of the district more than three decades ago he has demonstrated how private developments also conceived to improve public space can benefit both private and public interests. With this in mind, the 2017 expansion of the popular shopping and eating destination one block south along Fourth Street was intended to blur the distinction between public and private realms. A key concern for the project was the creation of additional off-street parking. The space behind the venerable Spenger's restaurant was the logical place for it. Out of the way of the shops and pedestrians, it provided a convenient location consistent with the developer's desire to create a lively car-free experience. This is now seamlessly connected to Fourth Street by a paseo that provides a garden setting, plenty of seating, and ample space for complementary outdoor activities.

In our design for this space we imagined how people stepping out of their cars might immediately enter an urban garden. The 104-car lot is thus shaded by a forest of spreading Chinese elm trees and edged with densely planted bioswales that filter and treat stormwater runoff. And from one of its corners it connects to the paseo that extends the dynamic experience of the current public shopping street. Lined with shops, eateries, maker shacks, performance spaces, seating, and plantings, this space on private property is open at all hours. It also provides a convenient mid-block connection between Fourth Street and an adjacent mixed-use residential area.

Configured as a linear plaza for people to pass through, the paseo also serves as an informal outdoor theater. Safely off the street visitors may sit there and watch a complex choreography unfold. Yet, as participants in the scene, they are both audience and performers. With entries and exits, textured pavement, interconnected rooms, festive lighting, greenery, and spaces for musicians, the space is deliberately composed for people to strut their stuff. What could have been an ordinary passageway between a parking lot and a city street thus becomes a place of rich landscape, human interaction, and enjoyment. It is a stage set designed to transport visitors to a special world.

Beneath the surface of the Paseo is also a drainage network that cleans and stores stormwater runoff from the paving and surrounding roof surfaces. The site, once a totally impermeable expanse of concrete and asphalt that sent polluted water racing unchecked into storm drains and San Francisco Bay, was transformed through the use of permeable paving and flow-through planters. These now recharge the groundwater and control the amount and quality of runoff released into the city's drains. However, this system, which is critical to the success of the flat site, is so closely integrated with the textured paving and lush planting beds that it is almost imperceptible.

The paseo is also located on what was once a larger bayfront settlement of the Ohlone people. And its east/west alignment reflects the natural flow of nearby Strawberry

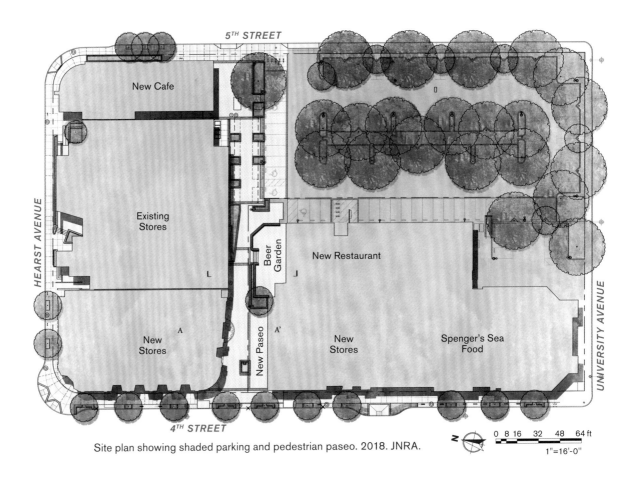

Site plan showing shaded parking and pedestrian paseo. 2018. JNRA.

The new Paseo is a modern-day urban response to the natural characteristics of the site that have informed humans settlements in this area for generations.

Creek, which once emptied into the Bay just to the south. The paseo thus likely also reflects thousands of years of travel between upland areas and the bayfront, connecting places for community gathering. In former times there likely would also have been places along this route to stop, protected from the westerly winds, to take in the sun and the natural setting.

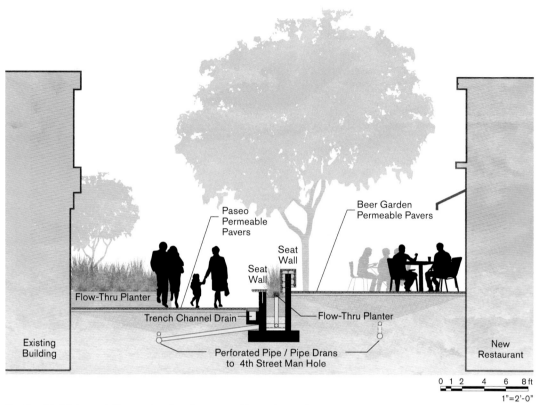

Section (A-A') through Paseo showing the permeable paving and stormwater management system. 2018. JNRA.

The paseo provides a modern-day urban response to the natural characteristics of the site, as these have informed human settlements in this area for generations.

This unique balancing of sustainable urban ecological systems and vibrant urban design was the first project of Daniela P. Corvillon's to be constructed since she joined my office. It marked the beginning of a long and fruitful association with a shared vision of the work that we do. ⊛

Following page: A place to see and be seen, the Paseo serves as an informal urban theater. 2018. Jose Luis Aranda.

ALMOST CLEAN
AND GREEN

NORTH WATERFRONT PARK & CESAR CHAVEZ MEMORIAL SOLAR CALENDAR
11 Spinnaker Way
Berkeley, CA

Right page: The Master Plan for North Waterfront Park reconfigures the 92-acre municipal landfill into a self-cleaning ecologically-based waterfront sanctuary. 1990. Richard Haag.

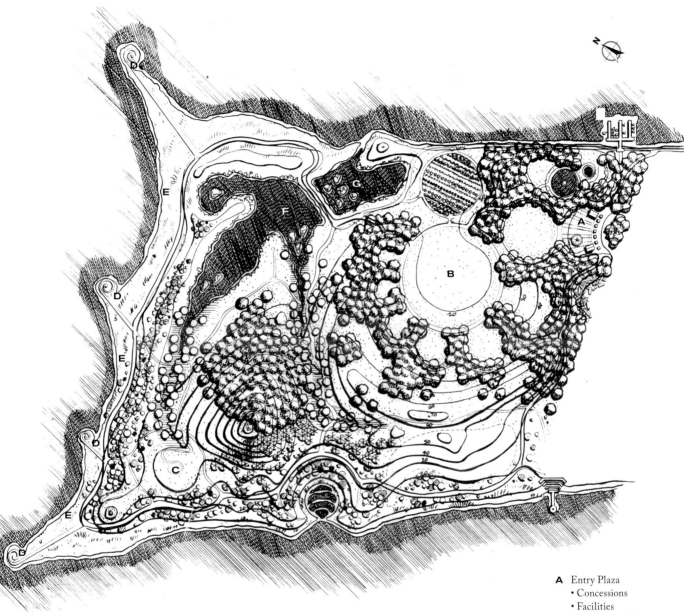

LANDFORM WATER TREES TRAILS

HAAG - ROBERTS - DENES Collaboration

A Entry Plaza
- Concessions
- Facilities
- Interpretive Center
- Kinetic Fountain

B Great Meadow
C View Mound
D Groins
E Beaches
F Freshwater Lake
G Brackish Marsh

0 100 200   400 ft

1"=100'

When challenging generally-accepted regulatory requirements and technologies, it is essential to get the underlying science and engineering right…

T his is the story of what I believe was a missed opportunity by the City of Berkeley to take an enlightened approach to resolving the serious ecological and pollution problems of a 92-acre municipal garbage dump on its shoreline. The approach may have seemed radical at the time, but the science and engineering underlying it have since become an accepted way to clean polluted brownfields across the world and restore them as productive lands.

I was hired by the city in 1987 to rewrite the master plan for North Waterfront Park, a park created on top of the giant pile of municipal garbage. My principal collaborator for the project would be Richard Haag, a renowned landscape architect from Seattle with extensive experience in the design of parks over toxic landfills including his city's internationally recognized Gasworks Park. Together, we approached the site as if it were an oversized rubbish-filled compost pile that could be cleaned up by enhancing natural process of decomposition. Instead of sealing it off with a clay cap as required by the powerful regulatory agencies, we thought the landscape systems of the park itself might be used as cleaning agents. We thus imagined opening the landfill, grinding and composting its organic matter, blending it with the clay cap to create healthy new soils, and then regrading the site. In this way the soil itself might provide the active medium for cleaning the landfill of gas and water pollutants — not just for growing plants.

Ultimately, the City of Berkeley's parks and engineering staff felt ill prepared to manage such a project. And despite strong community support, the Berkeley City Council reluctantly decided not to take a chance on our proposals. Instead, the city opted to install a standard methane flare system to burn off the landfill gases; it chose to continue trying to contain contaminated water within its perimeter levees; and it decided to maintain the surface improvements as they had been when the landfill was first sealed. This area is today a well-used and much-loved unstructured open space, sitting atop a mountain of slowly decomposing garbage. But I believe it could have been transformed by innovative processes into a much more environmentally benign, and ecologically rich place.

This story of what might have been is somewhat technical. When challenging accepted regulatory requirements and technologies it is essential to get the underlying science and engineering right. The plan we developed was built on a solid understanding of basic scientific and engineering principles, adapted to create what we believed would have been an ecologically sustainable place directly connected to its natural setting. The ideas we proposed are fascinating and achievable. Indeed, they are now being adapted at other contaminated sites.

Historic Context: As settlement expanded around the San Francisco Bay throughout the nineteenth and twentieth centuries, the area's burgeoning cities targeted the region's shallow bayfront marshes, beaches, and mud flats as opportunities to create new flat, developable land. This allowed the region's bayshore freeways to be built over mud flats

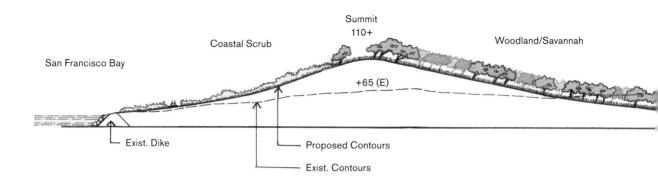

and marshes and entire new neighborhoods to be constructed on fill using soils excavated for development elsewhere and garbage dumped into diked enclosures. Thousands of acres of new land were created this way atop unstable bay mud. This massive act of ecological destruction was finally stopped in the late 1960s by community activists and state lawmakers — but only after most of the tidal marshes, beaches, and mud flats around San Francisco Bay, one of its richest and most diverse natural resources, had been buried.

North Waterfront Park, Berkeley's municipal dump, with garbage piled more than sixty feet high, was part of this heritage. The landfill was finally closed and sealed in the mid-1980s, as required by regional regulatory agencies. And after it was sealed with a clay cap it was opened to the public as a park named for the leader of the California farmworkers. The park's rolling landforms, plantings, pathways, and picnic areas were designed by city staff. And although on-site wetlands were promised in a future phase of the work, it was never clear how these would be created. The result was a pleasant, flexible-use grassy open space with a well-used perimeter trail and some experimental areas of native vegetation.

Controversy haunts every project in Berkeley, however, and this was no exception. Local environmental activists insisted that the park be redesigned to integrate community input, express its origins as a landfill, incorporate a seven-acre wetland/wildlife reserve, and reflect the natural ecological setting. I was selected as the prime consultant for this work, with Richard Haag as my primary design collaborator. Haag and I would form a lifelong professional relationship and personal friendship as a result of this project. Joining us in the work would be the chemical engineer Richard Brooks, a pioneer in the field of bioremediation.

Research: Before we could even consider beginning work on the redesign, we needed to understand the characteristics of the landfill, because these would provide a basis for all future considerations about management and park improvements. As a municipal dump, the site contained organic material as well as construction debris, discarded equipment, metals, and all manner of household refuse. Within its diked enclosure, the organic material would be slowly decomposing and producing landfill gases, primarily methane. The metals would

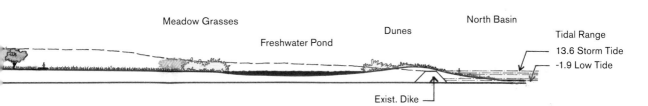

Diagrammatic cross section through the park showing proposed re-grading to create an ecological continuum from bayfront to hilltop. 1990. JNRA.

be slowly corroding, with their chemical components mixing with water trapped within the landfill to create leachate. The landfill gases and leachate, affecting both air and water quality, would be the principal pollutants we would have to address.

Methane is a major source of greenhouse gas pollution — more problematic than carbon dioxide, the primary culprit in global warming, but less common — and landfills are important methane producers. At the time we began our work, the city had yet to install a methane gas extraction and flare system to burn it off, as required by regulators. And we thought cleaning the site of methane would be better than burning it. To pursue that option, I contacted Sherwood Rowland, a research chemist at UC Irvine who would later win the Nobel Prize for his study of greenhouse gases. At that point Rowland had not yet thought of landfills as major contributors to greenhouse gases and global warming, but he was sufficiently interested to send a research associate to test our site for methane emissions. The tests confirmed that the landfill was producing large quantities of methane, as we expected, but we were surprised to find that only small amounts of the gas were escaping through the bare soil. It appeared as if something in the soil was consuming the methane.

Next we next took soil samples from the landfill and sent them to Rowland's colleagues at the University of Alaska who were studying the methane-consumption characteristics of tundra soils. Their scientific analysis confirmed that microbes in our soil, which they successfully isolated, were in fact actively consuming the methane. Indeed, if left to do their work, the scientists estimated that these microbes would be capable of removing a minimum of 70 percent of the methane produced by the landfill. Their study further included technical specifications for soils that might effectively remediate methane production while providing optimal conditions for plant growth. Eventually, their 1990 paper on the Berkeley North Waterfront Park landfill soils, "Rapid Methane Oxidation in a Landfill Cover Soil" was hailed as a breakthrough in bioremediation research. It has since been cited more than 400 times in other scientific papers. Indeed, it provides the basis for much of the bioremediation work happening throughout the world today.

The paper that was published on the
North Waterfront Park soils was
a breakthrough in bioremediation
research and has been cited in
subsequent scientific papers over
400 times.

Knowing that our theory of soil-based remediation of landfill gases was
scientifically sound, we next turned our attention to the potential of using the same soil to
remediate the organic pollutants found in the leachate that typically accumulates within
landfills. For this inquiry, we turned to the technology behind sanitary sewage treatment.

At the time there were real concerns about the leachate leaking through the
landfill's perimeter dikes and polluting San Francisco Bay. As a result, when water within
the landfill reached a certain height, the city would pump it out and dispose of it in a nearby
sanitary sewer. From there it would be piped to a sewage treatment plant, cleaned, and
discharged into the bay. We realized that, if the landfill's leachate could be satisfactorily
treated in a sewage treatment plant, a similar process might be employed using soils on site
— essentially using traditional leach field technology. This conclusion, however, flew in the
face of the established protocols of water-quality-control agencies. Regulators had previously
determined that the preferred method for dealing with leachate was to seal it off forever to
prevent its escape. But this was a practical impossibility for a landfill in a seismically active
intertidal zone that was gradually sinking into unstable bay mud. We suggested instead that
test plots be established to determine if an onsite soil-cleaning technique might also meet
water-quality standards. The community and scientists were interested, but the staff and
their engineers did not want to challenge the regulations.

Meanwhile, the question of whether there was a practical method for accelerating
the creation of soil from garbage was being answered by an innovative engineer overseeing
the landfills in Collier County, Florida. He had discovered that much of the organic
material in his landfills had decomposed and turned into soil. Since soil must be spread
over new garbage deposited in a landfill at the end of each day, and since obtaining this
soil is the most expensive part of operating a landfill, he had developed machinery that
would grind up the organic matter while separating out the inorganics. The ground-up

organic material could then be composted to accelerate the creation of soil. He had even founded a nonprofit entity to promote this technology. He estimated that the grinding and composting process could clean up Berkeley's entire 92-acre site within ninety days. By comparison, it would take at least one hundred years for the organic material in the presently sealed landfill to decompose. The engineer's alternative approach to waste disposal and recycling has now become commonplace, but it was rare at the time. We proposed additional test plots to explore the feasibility of mechanical excavation techniques.

Park Design: The scientific and engineering bases for cleaning the old garbage dump of its contaminants were clear. And with a clean site, there would be freedom to explore alternative ways to weave the land and its waterfrontage into an ecologically integrated place for both people and critters. For example, it might now be possible to create an ecological continuum on the former garbage dump from salt marsh to grasslands to wooded uplands. It might even be possible integrate freshwater marshes and riparian corridors. Although wetlands were not then allowed on landfills by the regulatory agencies, they might be used as a cleaning mechanism to further filter and polish treated water before recycling it back to the uplands for irrigation. And the soils excavated to create them might be used to build hills for upland forests, to create bioswales to control runoff, and to establish grassy meadows.

The landfill's transformation into a biological recovery station, to be incorporated gradually into the shapes and structures, biota and function of its whole environment, was enthusiastically supported by the community.

Before the filling of the bayfront, the Berkeley shoreline had also included an extensive sandy beach. Although the beach itself was long gone, there was ample evidence in surrounding areas that natural beach-building processes were still in effect. With proper engineering, it might thus be possible to recruit sediments around the edges of the landfill to re-create a self-sustaining beach there. And as an aid to this process, concrete construction rubble from the

Summer solstice sunset at the park. 2021. JNRA.

landfill could be strategically relocated to establish a pattern of revetments and bays that might slow the water, capture the sands, and allow to the building of beaches and dunes.

The landfill's transformation into a biological recovery station — to incorporate its shapes and structures, biota, and function as a whole environment — was a vision that was enthusiastically and unanimously supported by the community, scientists, and environmental activists. The plan was formally endorsed by the country's leading environmental organizations as well as by the most visionary environmental leaders of the time. But even if the community and scientists were interested in challenging the existing regulations, Berkeley's staff and their engineers were not. And in the end our proposals also proved too radical for Berkeley's political leaders. Nevertheless, they still provide a compelling image of how the detritus of our past might be used to create a place of reclaimed nature — and how the creative application of science and engineering may underlie the activity of placemaking.

Solar Calendar: Several years later, I was approached by Santiago Casal with a request to help him create a solar calendar and memorial to Cesar Chavez and Dolores

Huerta on the most remote hilltop in the park. This was the place we had identified in our plan that should be dedicated for community gatherings. It was a place we imagined where people might go to experience wild nature while gaining a panoramic understanding of our place within the regional landscape setting. A solar calendar at that location, to mark solstice and equinox alignments, might also help tie visitors to the cosmos and bridge cultures across the world. Coupled with a memorial to the great organizers of farmworkers, universal seasonal connections with agriculture could be made while honoring the community of ordinary people who do extraordinary things with their lives.

For more than thirty years, I have helped Santiago create this place of ritual gathering, education, connection with nature, and community bonds within the park. With gratitude for what we have been able to accomplish in the face of past hollow political rhetoric, searing disappointment, and finally acceptance, Jody and I also now visit the park regularly with our dog Lucy to enjoy the walks in the wind, the open space, and the vistas, while imagining even richer experiences. ⊙

Following page: Cesar Chavez Memorial Solar Calendar. 2021. Ashley James.

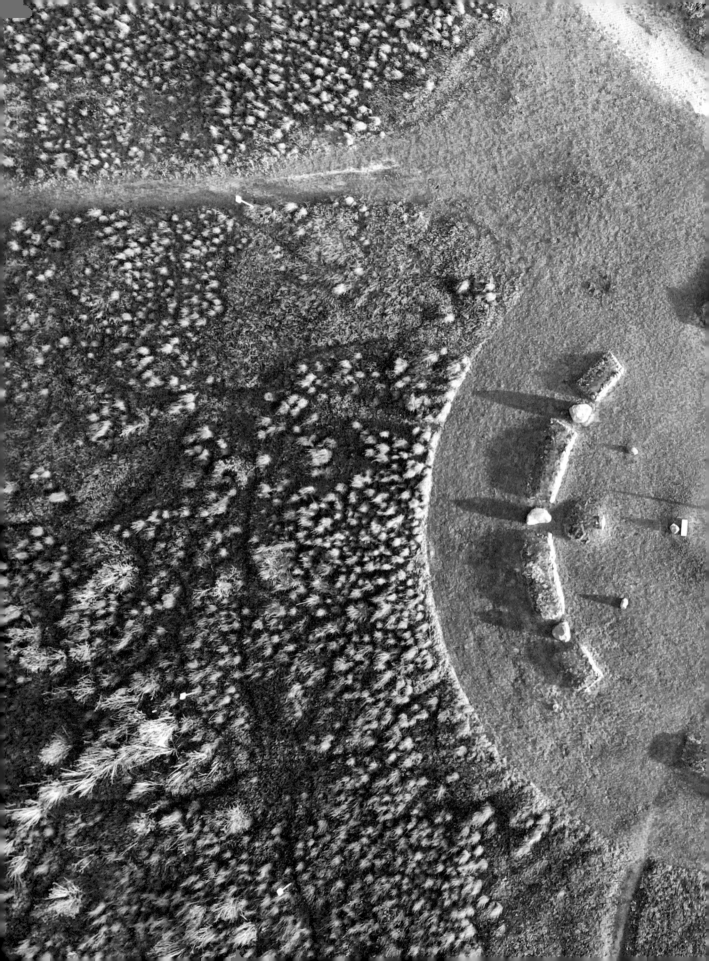

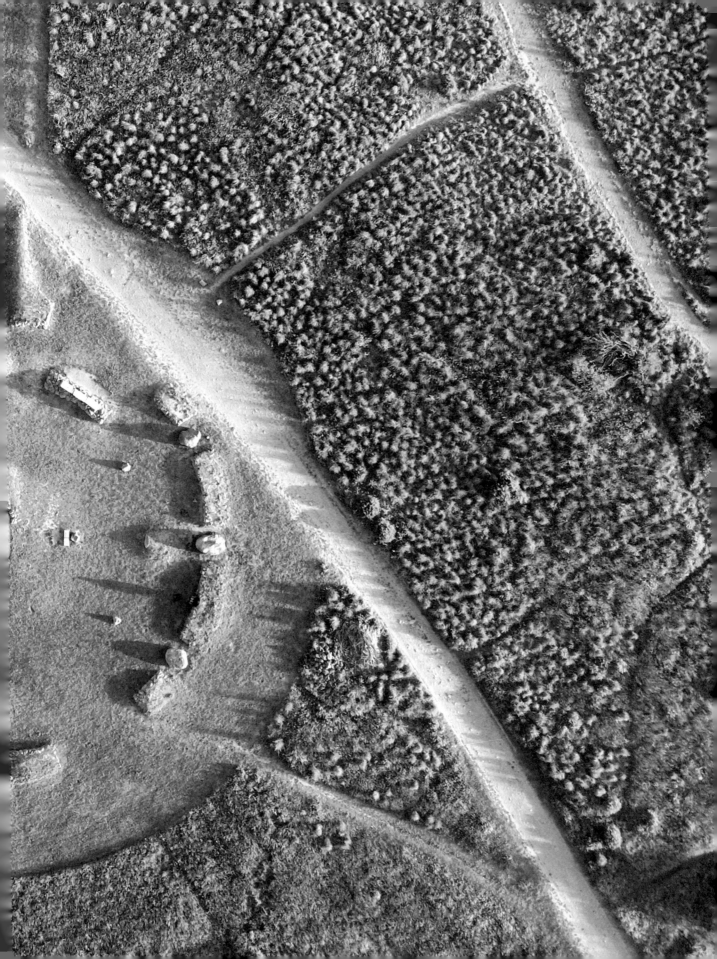

YOSEMITE VALLEY

THE HEART OF A PARK
Yosemite Village Day Use Area

MANAGING THE HORDES
Yosemite Lodge at the Falls

ACCESS TO WILDLANDS
Bridalveil Fall Access and Rehabilitation

Yosemite National Park, Mariposa County

YOSEMITE VALLEY

Yosemite Valley is a natural wonderland carved from the mountains by ancient glaciers and enclosed by sheer, 3,000-foot-high granite walls. Spectacular waterfalls cascade from the Sierra Nevada high country to fill a river that meanders over the valley floor through grand wet meadows, dense conifer forests, and ancient oak woodlands with abundant wildlife. The breathtaking beauty of the place is the result of eons of geologic activity locked in a dramatic, never-ending dance with water, in all its forms. Its result has been the sculpting of the fire-hardened rock into a series of iconic forms, including Half Dome, El Capitan, and Glacier Point, modern names ascribed within the last +/- 150 years. All mountain ranges are similarly formed, but few offer such picturesque and multilayered expressions of ecological forces. And the valley's remarkable vistas are but the opening expression of what many people — from early First Nation visitors to generations of naturalists and outdoor enthusiasts — have described as the far more profound experience embedded in the sensual and spiritual qualities of place.

Yosemite Valley was preserved for public use in 1864, years before the National Park Service (NPS) was created. But after 1890, when Yosemite National Park formally entered the U.S. park system, Yosemite Valley quickly became one of the most popular

Right page: Sketch of Yosemite Valley. 2021. Daniela P. Corvillon.

tourist destinations in the world. Yet, from the beginning as a park, people have been encouraged to visit, and the need to accommodate millions of visitors each year has resulted in an extensive built environment to support overnight and day use, a variety of recreational activities, and park operations and maintenance. Protecting the gift of the park itself while balancing visitor needs is an ongoing and complex urban/wildland management challenge.

Despite valiant efforts by NPS staff over the years, the problems of overcrowding, traffic jams, sprawling development, and overwhelmed infrastructure have for years been undermining the experience of this magical setting. Anyone who has sat through hours-long traffic jams at Yosemite Village and Yosemite Falls trying to leave the valley on a Sunday afternoon, or who has battled the crowds on the steep, narrow trails to the falls, or who has endured the noxious odors and long lines at the poorly ventilated, overused vault toilets has had to wonder what happened to the Eden-like qualities they expected to experience in the valley.

> The breathtaking natural beauty is a result of eons of geologic activity locked in a dramatic never-ending dance with water, in all its forms, sculpting the fire-hardened earth to create an ecological wonderland.

The devastating 1997 flood of the Merced River provided a dramatic wakeup call. Large portions of Yosemite Lodge, much of the roadway through the valley, and other developments within the floodplain were wiped out. Emergency repairs followed, but long-overdue infrastructure improvements to help manage the hordes of people and their vehicles coming to the valley year-round were also critical. Those improvements, however, could not be made until an acceptable Park Management Plan was adopted. Empowered by environmental legislation and an increased ecological consciousness in the culture, interested citizens, environmental organizations, people of the First Nations, and others had been pressuring the NPS to develop an ecologically and culturally responsive plan that would shift park priorities to more stringent environmental protections. Institutional change was slow and difficult, but it was gradually being realized.

Left page: Yosemite Valley from Tunnel View with Bridalveil Fall on the right, Half Dome in the center distance, and El Capitan on the left. 2015. JNRA.

It was not until 2014 (seventeen years after the flood) that the Merced River Plan (MRP) was subsequently approved. The health of the river would be the paramount consideration for any changes proposed within the valley, a paradigm shift that was now fully embraced by the NPS. The MRP set out to address specific conflicts and provide a comprehensive valley-wide framework for rebalancing the natural and built environments. The MRP now mandates that all structures built within the floodplain of the Merced River be removed or relocated and that an extensive campaign be undertaken to restore riverine habitats. It directs that day-use parking, bus parking, and related facilities be redistributed throughout the valley to relieve the concentrated impacts at primary destinations. And it specifies that improvements be made to the one-way loop road around the valley to reduce congestion, delays, air pollution, noise, and conflicts between vehicles, pedestrians, and bicyclists. In addition, the designation of the Merced River as a Wild and Scenic River will bring strict management requirements related to visitor use, pollution, wildlife corridors, congestion and overcrowding of trails, and destructive off-trail activity.

Once the MRP was approved, it became possible to address a thirty-year backlog of delayed infrastructure projects, and we were hired to address several knotty issues at the interface between the valley's built and natural environments. The first of these was to design a new point of visitor arrival at Yosemite Village. The second was to provide a comprehensive site-development plan for the Lodge at Yosemite Falls to sort out complex transportation conflicts and visitor use requirements in response to flood damage, the new floodplain restrictions of the MRP, and the new public access directives of the MRP. An expansion of the Camp 4 campground was included as part of this project. The last project we were assigned was to create a plan for the rehabilitation of the Bridalveil Fall area and recreational access to the fall.

Yosemite Valley is a place for recreational tourists to visit and for pilgrims to celebrate. It is a sacred landscape of water and fire. It is also a place where complex, pressing ecological urban and community design issues required resolution within the framework of a new and equitable socio-ecological ethic. ⊛

Left page: The Merced River is designated a Wild and Scenic River, the ecological centerpiece for management of the valley. 2022. JNRA.

THE HEART OF
A PARK

YOSEMITE VILLAGE DAY-USE AREA
Yosemite Village, Yosemite Valley
Yosemite National Park, CA

Right page: Developments at Yosemite Village that encroached on the Merced River have been moved out of the floodplain. 2014. JNRA.

The primary point of arrival for Park visitors offers a welcoming, rich, and educational landscape experience that reflects the power of the setting while protecting the forests, wetlands, river, and vistas. This could not simply be a place to store vehicles for the day.

Yosemite Village is the heart of Yosemite Valley, serving both as the primary destination for tens of thousands of daily visitors and the operational center of the park. It sits in a forest just above the Merced River on the sunny side of the valley, contained comfortably within the embrace of the surrounding granite walls and featuring dramatic long views of the valley rim. The village is bracketed by tributary streams that flow from waterfalls to nearby wet meadows and the river beyond. The defining landscape features of Yosemite Valley – river, wetlands, falls, meadows, forests, granite cliffs - are all part of this specific place. Also located here are the Park Headquarters, Visitor Center, a post office, museums, retail shops, a grocery store and deli, park maintenance and operations facilities, a medical clinic, concessionaire offices, a hotel, a jail, staff housing, and all the infrastructure needed to support these uses - an urban hub in a wildland setting.

Unfortunately, the wondrous and rich sense of arrival that visitors once experienced at the village had seriously deteriorated over time. After enduring hours-long traffic jams, visitors would typically be greeted by confusing parking arrangements, dangerous road crossings, congestion, poor signage, limited orientation measures, an absence of restrooms, occasional flooding, encroachments into the river floodplain, and a generally compromised natural setting. This is a story about the experience of arrival at a place.

Following approval of the Merced River Plan (MRP), a top priority for park management was to address the suite of problems at Yosemite Village. The day-use parking lot would need to be relocated out of the Merced River floodplain. The loop roadway serving the entire valley would need to be realigned to eliminate the unsafe pedestrian crossing between the main parking lot and village trails. A roundabout would need to be built at the village entrance to relieve the miles-long traffic backup caused by an inefficient four-way stop. Publicly accessible restrooms were needed to serve the large number of day-use visitors. And additional parking, roadway, and shuttle-bus improvements were necessary in association with future building removals within the village area.

Park management and staff saw an opportunity to leverage the necessary roadway engineering and parking lot improvements to create a new point of visitor arrival offering a welcoming, rich, and educational experience that would reflect the power of the setting while protecting the forests, wetlands, river, and vistas. As the first major project to be built under the new MRP these parking lots could no longer simply be considered a place to store vehicles for the day. With the recommendation of park staff, we were hired by the Federal Highway Administration's engineering firm to design an ecologically based visitor-arrival experience. Our scope of work included redesigning and expanding the parking lots; improving trail connections; locating the new restrooms; designing shuttle stops, gathering areas, and interpretive facilities; and ensuring adequate wetland and forest protections. The engineers would produce the final construction documents from our plans. We were flattered, excited, skeptical, and humbled to be chosen to work in Yosemite.

ARRIVAL AT THE HEART

YOSEMITE VILLAGE

VALLEY BIKE TRAIL

Reconfigured Parking Lots 320 Cars

AHWAHNEE MEADOW

Visitor Contact Station

COOKS MEADOW

(E) and Restored Wetland

Indian Creek

VALLEY BIKE TRAIL

← To Swinging Bridge

NEW TRAIL CONNECTIONS

(E) Wetland

Comfort Station

Shuttle Stop

ARRIVAL PLAZA

New Parking 400 Cars

MERCED RIVER

Additional Restored Wetland

2yr Floodplain

Edge of Former Parking Lot

0 50 100   200   300   400 ft

1"=100'

Site Plan for the Yosemite Village Parking area showing redesigned roadway and parking, arrival plaza, trail connections, preserved forests, and restored wetlands. 2015. JNRA.

From the outset, the park managers told us they did not want to be sued for violation of the MRP, which they were sure would happen if they followed the engineer's original plans. Indeed, the deputy superintendent introduced herself at our first meeting with the unsettling comment that the work we were about to begin was the only item in planning for the valley that had not been litigated over the past thirty years, so we had better get it right. The Yosemite Village point of arrival was a strategically important target of the MRP.

The confusion, discomfort, and disorientation produced by the former parking lots has now been replaced with a simple, clear, and comfortable arrival experience shaped to respect the river's natural pattern of flow and to help visitors understand where they are. Realigning the roadway and relocating the parking areas were the key changes. The parking was moved out of the floodplain to the village side of the realigned road, eliminating conflicts with the pedestrian crossing and allowing traffic and the river to flow unimpeded around the parking lot. And a new roundabout was constructed at the main village intersection, allowing through-traffic to continue without stopping — a major cause of valley-wide traffic back-ups. By relocating the road and moving the parking out of the Merced River floodplain, the area of the former parking lot has been restored as riverside wetlands. Likewise, the former roadbed has been repurposed for trail connections, wetland restoration, and reforestation.

The new parking lot design preserved all the existing black oak trees as well as more than 95 percent of the area's other trees, integrating the existing forests as visual and ecological buffers. The new configuration also allowed the preservation and enhancement of an additional 3.5 acres of wetlands along the tributary streams flowing through the village area — wetlands the MRP had assumed would have to be sacrificed to the new parking lots. These expanded wetlands and areas of preserved forest at the urbanized village now greet visitors, furthering the incremental ecological restoration of the valley beyond what was imagined in the MRP and helping to rebalance nature and the built environment. People arrive at a place of nature where the forces that have created this landscape are fully integrated with the built environment at this new point of arrival. Looking down from Glacier Point after the changes were complete, the once-skeptical deputy superintendent remarked that the new parking lot fit seamlessly into its setting. And, sighing with relief, she noted that no one has been sued.

Within the parking lot the design of the arrival plaza works in conjunction with a new comfort station. From that location, visitors can orient themselves to the larger context of the place through framed views of Half Dome and other iconic features around the valley's rim. Following clear signage from this central hub they can also explore a wheel-and-spoke system of trails providing access to Yosemite Village, a nearby valley shuttle-bus stop, Cook's Meadow, and more distant attractions. The connecting pathways follow the tributary streams and their associated wetlands into the village or out to destinations elsewhere in the valley, engaging visitors immediately with the water-based ecology of the valley floor. The initial

Following page: Trails from the Village Day Use Parking Lot lead visitors along water courses to and around the meadows. 2021. JNRA.

arrival experience thus introduces visitors both to the vistas and underlying ecology of the place while seamlessly taking care of human needs. There is much to explore, but the essence of the place can be discovered once the visitor exits their vehicle.

The new village day-use area, with its roadway realignment, parking lots, trail links, and arrival plaza, reflects the abstract form of a living heart, with inflows into chambers and outflows to the body — a fitting metaphor for the primary arrival point within Yosemite

The arrival plaza orients visitors to the landscape setting while serving visitor needs with a comfort station, seating, picnic areas, trail connections, and interpretive panels that screen the parking. 2022. JNRA.

Valley and the inherent life force of this place. This new relationship between the built
and natural environment can serve as a model for other projects, leading incrementally to
significant valley-wide improvements. Only time will tell, however, if such clever, ecologically
driven urban design will be enough to protect the integrity of the park's gifts for generations
to come, or if more stringent measures will be required to limit the impacts caused by the
great numbers of visitors currently allowed. ⊛

MANAGING
THE HORDES

YOSEMITE LODGE AT THE FALLS
Yosemite Valley
Yosemite National Park, CA

Right page: Yosemite Lodge sits within the forest near the base of Yosemite Falls just above the Merced River with trail connections to the meadows and mountains. 2022. JNRA.

The Lodge could not be rebuilt within the floodplain as it had been before. A new comprehensive site plan was required to re-imagine the Lodge developments and public uses.

Yosemite Lodge was built in the 1950s as a destination motel near the base of, but across the loop road from, Yosemite Falls, the most dramatic of the many waterfalls in Yosemite Valley and one of the valley's most popular visitor destinations and photo opportunities. It was also located next to one of the valley's premier archeological resources: the site of the principal village built in the valley by its first inhabitants, the Native Ahwanechee (Miwok) people. This was, and continues to be, the logical site for human settlement in the valley — on the valley's sunny side for warmth in winter, under spreading black oak trees whose acorns were a staple food source, on high ground near the spectacular waterfall, and overlooking wet meadows filled with wildlife.

Yosemite Lodge was originally built as a private commercial concession to serve paying overnight customers, with limited facilities for the general public. But the increasing popularity of Yosemite Falls as a day-use destination was putting a serious strain on the capacity of the lodge to serve the needs both of its guests and the public at large. In particular, the lodge grounds had become the primary destination for tour buses, regional transit buses, park-wide shuttles, and popular in-valley open-air trams. While the use of buses and shuttles was promoted by park management as a way to limit the use of private vehicles in the valley, the haphazard accommodation of the large transit vehicles, which released periodic pulses of visitors, created conditions that were confusing, and dangerous. Without clear loading and unloading areas, the shared use of lodge parking lots by buses and other visitors led to significant conflicts between lodge operations, guests, and day-use visitors.

In addition to the internal transportation conflicts within the Yosemite Lodge site, the day-use and tour bus visitors walking across the loop road from the lodge to Lower Yosemite Falls were contributing to serious valley-wide traffic congestion, with delays on the roadway at peak times sometimes causing tempers to flare. However, a rerouting of the roadway so that visitors would not have to cross it — as was done at Yosemite Village — would not work here because it would conflict with the river floodplain and potentially require the removal of historically significant buildings. Of all the problems faced at Yosemite Lodge, this was the most vexing. This is a story about creating order from chaos while rediscovering nature in a domesticated wildland setting.

More than half of the sprawling complex of buildings, roads, and parking lots at the lodge had been wiped out in the 1997 flooding of the Merced River. But approval of the Merced River Plan (MRP) in 2014 finally allowed critical changes to begin. The MRP, however, mandated that rebuilding within the floodplain where structures had stood before would not be allowed. NPS realized that a comprehensive new site plan was therefore needed to reimagine the lodge, its surrounding developments, and associated public uses. My office was asked to develop this new site plan. We would be subconsultants to Siegel & Strain Architects, who had a master contract for work in Yosemite from the National

FROM CHAOS TO ORDER IN A NATURAL LANDSCAPE

To El Capitan

UPPER YOSEMITE
FALL TRAIL

Camp 4

Camp 4
Expansion

Parking Lot 130 Cars

Restoration

NEW ENTRY

TRANSIT HUB

ARRIVAL
PLAZA

Day Use Parking 300 Cars

100 Year
Flood Line

Bus Parking 24 Buses

Housekeeping

2yr
Floodplain

(E) Wetland

to Swinging Bridge,
BBQ Area and Beach

MERCED RIVER

0 50 100   200   300   400 ft

1"=100'

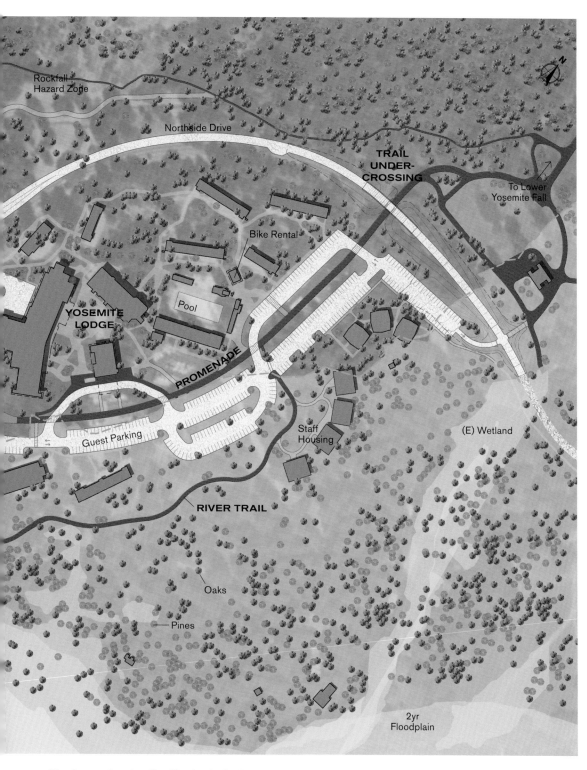

The Comprehensive Site Plan for the Lodge area reorganizes transportation systems, parking, and trails to create a safe, conflict-free, and resource-rich visitor experience. 2016. JNRA.

The urban systems must work and not get in the way of the park experience - they must both support visitors' needs and complement the natural resources, the essence of urban ecological design.

Park Service. As of this writing, only portions of the approved lodge site plan have been implemented, so it is only possible to describe its key elements, its intent as adopted, and some of the underlying considerations.

The biggest change incorporated in the redesign involved shoehorning a high-impact, highly visible transit hub into the lodge area. Such a facility was needed as the park was strongly encouraging bus access over private vehicles, and it had to be located in an efficient, central location in a way that did not conflict with other activities or modes of transportation. The resolution of this complex ecological/urban design challenge would also need to complement the park arrival experience without compromising the natural or historic setting. As a stand-alone facility, the transit hub would need to accommodate multiple large buses requiring generous maneuvering room; it would need easy access from the roadway; and it would need to provide ample space for passenger loading and unloading. The primary point of arrival in the valley for many visitors, it also would require a gracious gathering area, orientation and interpretive displays, and public restroom facilities. Finally,

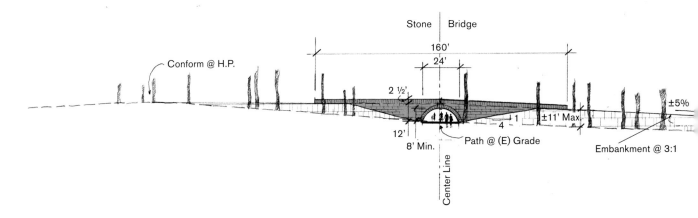

Diagrammatic cross section/elevation showing the proposed elevated perimeter roadway and trail under-crossing to eliminate the traffic conflict. 2015. JNRA.

a remote area for storing buses for several hours while the passengers visited the park was needed, sited away from the lodge and trails.

The site of a temporary staff housing complex was ultimately selected as the location for the transit hub. This was directly accessible from the perimeter road, near the core of the lodge area, but along one of its forested edges. We discovered this could be configured to save most of the trees while handling nine buses plus an additional three overflow spaces, for a total of twelve buses at one time — the maximum number anticipated by park management to meet future needs. A tree-shaded plaza with restrooms could also be created here with a direct connection to a new pedestrian promenade and a view of Lower Yosemite Falls. This new complex would thus organize the existing chaotic, ad-hoc bus service area into a coherent, safe arrival space in a parklike setting, while offering visitors pedestrian access to the center of the lodge complex and trails.

The site design also created an expanded day-use parking area, as recommended in the Merced River Plan to disperse day-use visitors throughout the valley. A large new parking lot was created on the forested western edge of the lodge complex, which would also provide visually buffered space for the temporary storage of 24 buses while they awaited their return passengers. Visitors who parked in this new 300-vehicle day-use parking lot would also have convenient access to new restrooms, orientation information, and trails.

The primary destination for the throngs of day-use and transit visitors in the area would continue to be the Lower Yosemite Falls Trail. Consolidation of the lodge guest parking and service roads, conversion of a secondary roadway for pedestrian use, and relocation of the buses would create space for a generous promenade through the center of lodge complex. This safe pedestrian path would seamlessly link the arrival plazas, Yosemite Lodge, Yosemite Falls, and other public destinations in the area, while offering stunning views of the falls.

Access to the Lower Yosemite Falls Trail currently requires that visitors cross the loop roadway, causing a traffic delay that ripples throughout the entire valley. This is especially the

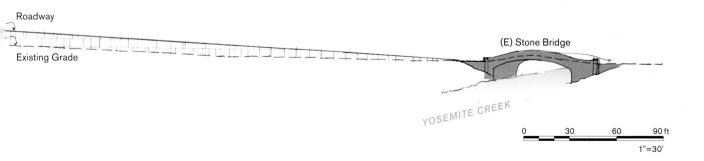

The new promenade would seamlessly link the arrival plaza, the Lodge, the Falls, and other public uses along a safe pedestrian path through the landscape with stunning views of the Falls.

case near the end of the day when many visitors are heading home. A conflict-free road crossing was sorely needed to resolve the single worst traffic problem in the valley. Our proposal was to raise the road and continue the promenade to the Lower Falls Trail at existing grade underneath a new stone roadway bridge of the kind commonly found throughout the valley. The separation would allow both the road and the promenade to function uninterrupted without conflicting with each other, eliminating the traffic bottleneck and minimizing the visual impact.

The modification of the existing roadway to create the pedestrian underpass would require relatively simple engineering — steepening the incline and building an archway over the promenade, while being careful to minimize disturbances to the archeological site. The roadway reconfiguration would require that the main vehicular entry for the lodge complex be relocated to a spot near the day-use parking area and transit hub. This solution was enthusiastically endorsed by the park staff and park management with agreement from the concessionaire, and preliminary engineering design was completed. However, further progress has been delayed until historic and archeological resource studies are completed, funding is secured, and park leadership recommits itself to solving these problems.

The intensity of activity, high number of visitors, and density of development at Yosemite Lodge demands a higher level of investment in the built environment than typically warranted in a wildland park area. However, the MRP recognizes the need for such intense developments in select locations within the valley. Our view was that the urban systems must work efficiently, but that they must not get in the way of the park experience. They must support visitors' needs, complement the natural resources, and create a sustainable balance between the built and natural environments: the essence of urban ecological design. These developments at the lodge may one day provide a key part of a system-wide effort to support a broader set of environmental goals for the valley as a whole: to protect and enhance the natural flow of the Merced River while improving the visitor experience at each destination within it. ⊛

Left page: The parking will be replaced with a pedestrian promenade through the Lodge complex and under the perimeter roadway to connect with the Lower Yosemite Valls trail. 2016. JNRA.
Following page: The Yosemite Lodge site plan protects the Merced River floodplain from developments while providing controlled recreational access to the river. 2022. JNRA.

ACCESS TO WILDLANDS

BRIDALVEIL FALL ACCESS AND REHABILITATION
Yosemite Valley
Yosemite National Park, CA

Right page: Bridalveil Fall cascades 600' from a hanging valley in the high-country into a boulder field at the upper overlook. 2016. JNRA.

Making the overlook at the base of Bridalveil Fall safe and accessible to all had become a primary goal of the Park management, although the accessibility goal was eventually scaled back.

C ascading waters at Bridalveil Fall crash into a bowl of giant boulders just above a visitor overlook before they spill into rock-strewn channels that weave through the forest to the Merced River below. Breezes waft the falling water into a diaphanous veil across the more than 600-foot-high granite face, sending mists into the lush wetland and boulder fields of the side canyon. When the high-country snowmelt is at its peak, these mists also shower the overlook, cleansing visitors who have carried the tensions of their daily lives to the park. Immersed in the powerful watery experience, with all their senses activated, visitors have no choice but to concentrate on being in that moment in that specific landscape. Afterwards, I've watched as they return down the trail to their vehicles, soaked to the skin, but transported, their scowls replaced by smiles and laughter. The sensual experience of that place is one that people carry with them for the rest of their lives. Their relationship with nature may be forever changed.

When visitors arrive at Yosemite Valley, Bridalveil Fall is the first major wildland feature they encounter where they can get out of their vehicles after hours of driving and personally engage with nature. All visitors to the valley pass Bridalveil, with most stopping to walk to the overlook at the dramatic base of the falls. After only a short quarter-mile hike, which rises just more than 80 vertical feet from the parking lot, Bridalveil Fall offers an intimate connection with wild nature without needing to travel to a pristine, out-of-the-way place. It may be overrun with throngs of visitors, but it still offers an unparalleled wildland experience. This is a story about accessibility in wildlands.

The National Park Service (NPS) actively encourages people to visit Bridalveil Fall, but because the overlook does not meet accessibility standards, it presents a potential violation of federal and state law and the civil rights of people with mobility impairments. Unlike many of the other natural sites in Yosemite Valley, however, its location holds great potential for making the transformational experience of visiting it available to people of all physical abilities. Making the overlook at the base of Bridalveil Fall safe and accessible for all was initially a primary goal of the rehabilitation work that park management intended for the site. However, as this work proceeded, the accessibility goal was scaled back for several reasons that I hope may one day be reevaluated.

We were hired by the Yosemite Conservancy to develop plans, through an extensive public outreach process, for the rehabilitation of the Bridalveil Fall area. The conditions in the visitor arrival area and along the overlook trail had deteriorated badly. The talented new NPS Project Manager, Brad Lewis, would oversee the rehabilitation design and construction process. We were charged with developing plans to reduce crowding on the trail, discourage rampant destructive use of off-trail areas, replace the restrooms, renovate the parking, reduce flooding in the parking lot, create a welcome point of arrival at the parking lot and at a new tour bus stop along the roadway, and create a legally compliant accessible route to the fall overlook.

The general site rehabilitation would require upgraded toilets and a renovated parking/arrival area to address the most frequent visitor complaints. The four existing poorly ventilated, vault-style toilets were insufficient for the thousands of daily visitors, and long queues to use them prompted many visitors to seek relief on the hillside. "French flowers," the name rangers gave the deposits of toilet paper and their associated "fertilizer," could be found throughout the heavily damaged off-trail areas. Replacement of the vault toilets with flush toilets, and an increase in their number, would require a new water well and a mile-long sanitary sewer line. In addition, chronic flooding of the low-lying parking lot and an inefficient parking layout presented further problems that required correction.

The small overlook at the base of the fall and the narrow, steep connecting trail were particularly problematic. Both were dangerously overcrowded, especially during the months when the waterfall was running at its highest levels and during freezing weather, making them extremely slippery and among the most hazardous facilities in the park. The steepness of the trail also far exceeded all accessibility standards, preventing any but the heartiest of movement-impaired visitors from getting to the base of the fall. Meanwhile, the crowds of people on the single, "cul-de-sac" trail encouraged many to strike off cross-country, trampling

vegetation and disturbing the wetlands. Overcrowding and inaccessibility thus raised complex
questions about resource protections, appropriate levels of improvement, and compliance with
accessibility laws.

Our highest priority would be to explore the feasibility of a new trail for all
visitors from the parking lot to the upper overlook at the base of the fall. We found that a
traditionally designed, legally compliant, at-grade trail through the boulder fields, wetlands,
and forest would be so tortured and disruptive that the park staff was prepared to close the
overlook altogether as a way of complying with accessibility laws. However, no one wanted
to close the overlook. The powerful experience at the base of the fall was too compelling and
complementary to the mission of the park, and the site was so popular that it would have
been impossible to keep visitors away. We were instructed by the park and the Conservancy
to expand our thinking to find a way to make the overlook accessible while reducing
overcrowding by dispersing visitors onto a new "loop" trail.

To create the loop, a new trail would have to traverse the dynamic boulder-strewn
wetlands, however, while having only minimal impact on the landscape nurtured by mist
from the fall. We proposed a sinuous elevated structure that would bridge over the boulder

Wetlands formed by the mist of the Fall within a boulder field create a lush and richly textured landscape
experience. 2016. JNRA.

A new accessible trail and mid-level overlook features views of the Fall. 2016. Rendering by Al Forster.

A sinuous elevated structure to bridge over the boulder fields and wetlands and land opportunistically at solid high ground would not be a traditional Yosemite structure.

fields and wetlands and land opportunistically on solid high ground. This would not be a traditional Yosemite structure. Rather, it would make use of a simple self-supporting metal bridging system, tied into boulders for support, to climb at a gentle, accessible gradient. The use of modular lightweight elements would limit disturbance to the wetlands by reducing the need for heavy equipment during construction. It was an ecologically and socially responsible design that would meet the goals of the project. However, it proved too radical a change for the park to accept.

The proposed arrival plaza with a new restroom building and redesigned parking greet visitors with a direct view of the Fall. 2016. Rendering by Al Forster.

Our proposal was ultimately rejected by park management after a years-long consensus-based design process based on opposition from park operations staff and the in-house trails crew assigned the task of constructing and maintaining the trail. Instead of our proposed design, they insisted that the elevated portions of the trail be like other structures that appeared in Yosemite. This traditional form was what the trails crew had expertise in building on relatively flat sites: heavy straight bridge segments with 40-foot-long steel I-beams set on massive concrete spread footings excavated into the wetlands. The park's response thus represented a clear rejection of an unfamiliar, nontraditional, and innovative resolution of a multifaceted problem. Fundraising for such a new structure was an added concern of the Conservancy. Ultimately, given the complexity of the terrain and the limitations of the acceptable construction technology, the goal of whole-access to the upper overlook and a rare wilderness experience for all was abandoned in favor of an accessible intermediate-level lookout offering a good photo opportunity.

The debate about accessibility in a wildland environment is complex. Bridalveil's hazardous and degraded site could be repaired and brought into compliance with accessibility laws with minimal environmental intrusion. But the possibility of doing so raised questions about appropriate levels of disabled access in wildlands. More important than aesthetics, the staff argued that such a structure would create an unnecessary intrusion into the natural

Key NPS staff argued successfully that accommodation of accessibility in this case was an unnecessary and irreparable intrusion into that natural environment.

environment for a limited purpose: that the park should protect mobility-impaired people from potentially dangerous experiences instead of finding ways for them to safely join. Ironically, on that very same day of our presentation, the annual Para-Olympic Games were under way with ability-impaired athletes accomplishing incredible feats and challenging preconceived notions of what was possible. Park management, by contrast, was clearly not ready to fully embrace the idea of whole access, and we were not able to convince them otherwise.

Our final design included an accessible first phase boardwalk of traditional design through the lower elevation wetlands. An accessible loop trail to the upper overlook will have to wait for a future round of improvements. Trail installation proceeded over the next three years under Brad Lewis's close supervision. As part of the new trail work, the existing upper overlook was expanded to ease overcrowding and its steep trail link modified slightly to make it a little safer. In addition, a separate accessible trail connection and point of arrival serving a new bus parking area was created along the entry road.

As the final engineering plans were being completed, the operations staff insisted that the restroom building be moved from the edge of the forest to an island in the middle of the parking lot, which they argued would be easier to maintain, cheaper to build, and less likely to be damaged. It would also be the first thing for visitors see, instead of the falls, and would organize visitor activities in the middle of the parking lot rather than safely to the side. The park superintendent decided the restrooms would go where the maintenance staff wanted them even though this site contradicted years of consensus planning, was inconsistent with design guidelines, and involved a costly last-minute change.

Sometimes, our design proposals are not acceptable to those in charge, and we must live with that. It was clear that the values we brought to the project were now out of sync with those of park management and our Conservancy client. Which voice would be our guide? Places are created as a reflection of the collective values of the communities responsible for them. Bittersweetly, we decided to part company. But circumstances can change. I am hopeful that at some future time, when I am wheelchair-bound but still want to immerse myself in a wildland experience, I will be able to get myself to the base of Bridalveil Fall. ⊛

Right page: The upper overlook at the base of the Fall will be enlarged to better accommodate the crowds. 2016. Rendering by Al Forster.

GATEWAY
Redwood National and State Parks Visitor Center

Redwood National
and State Parks,
Humboldt County

GATEWAY

REDWOOD NATIONAL AND STATE PARKS VISITOR CENTER
Bald Hills Road at Highway 101
Orick, CA

Right page: The Visitor Center site in the distance surrounded by forest is at the threshold of the North Coast Redwood Region three miles north of the town of Orick. 2015. JNRA.

The site will serve as the gateway to the region - a dramatic reshaping of the land to create a place where the wild forces of nature and the built human environment will co-exist in harmony, each sustaining the other.

This is the story of the transformation of a degraded former lumber mill site into a gateway to the natural wonders of Humboldt County on California's North Coast, a region known for its scenic coastline, rugged mountains, and majestic coast redwood forests. The site is located three miles upstream from the small town of Orick at the confluence of Prairie and Redwood Creeks. In former times this was a place of incredibly rich biological diversity and complex cultural heritage. Here, two streams converged at the edge of what was once an extensive forest that provided a home for a variety of wildlife, including elk, bear, deer, and the endangered marbled murrelet. It was also a place of residence of the Native Yurok people, for whom the European concept of north was not a cardinal direction but meant upstream, in whatever direction that led. The abundant water, rich soils, and coastal climate created conditions that supported life in layered interdependence, and the streams were its lifeblood.

Beginning in the mid-nineteenth century, however, farmers and loggers of European descent displaced the Yurok people from this place and changed its landscape. At first they cut the trees in the immediate area for building material and to create pastures in which to graze cattle. But a lumber mill was then built to process old-growth redwoods and Douglas fir from the surrounding forests on a far larger scale. Up to ten feet of river-run gravel was first placed on the site to raise it above routine flood levels and it was then paved over with asphalt to facilitate the mill's operation. The nearby delta, where the two creeks joined in a dynamic seasonal dance, was tamed with levees to protect the roads leading to the site and beyond. As a consequence of these activities the once abundant salmon runs in both Prairie and Redwood Creeks diminished to a mere fraction of their former glory.

Thus situated at the junction of the two streams, the mill survived for sixty years. But it finally succumbed to the pressure of fearless protestors who chose to place their bodies in harm's way to protect the area's remaining old-growth redwoods, the largest of which may still be found just upstream. Redwood National Park was also created nearby in 1968, and it was expanded in 1978 in response to the public outcry. Following the closure of the mill, the families of the former loggers and mill workers struggled to make ends meet while they waited for the long-delayed recreational tourist boom to begin.

In 2013, the mill was finally abandoned, and its badly degraded 125-acre site was purchased by the Save the Redwoods League, which was intent on restoring its ecological health, creating a new visitor center for the nearby Redwood National and State Parks, and transferring the entire property to the National Park Service. Their hope was that such a facility might serve as a gateway for recreational and educational use of the region while providing a living example of ecological restoration harmoniously balanced with human use. We were hired by the League as part of a team assembled by Siegel & Strain Architects that was tasked with developing a holistic site plan, designing a new visitor center complex, and collaborating on the site restoration. As part of this effort we would need to work closely

Reviewing the site analysis with the Yurok Tribal Chairman at the Visitor Center site. 2016. JNRA.

with the community of Orick, the Yurok Tribe, the State and National Parks, and the League to create a place to serve all users.

The long-term project as presently conceived integrates a new visitor center complex with the restoration of Prairie Creek. Its overall goal is to reestablish the natural continuum from the creek channel and floodplain through the adjacent upland meadows and forests to the remnant stands of old-growth redwoods while harmoniously accommodating visitors. The visitor center would be sited in the ecological transition area between the restored uplands and the old growth forest as the primary point of public access. While this whole project will not be completed for many years, the ideas behind it are sufficiently compelling to warrant telling the story of the long-range vision for this unusual place. It represents an example of how the land may be reshaped to create a place where the wild forces of nature and the built human environment coexist seamlessly, each sustaining the other. By the year 2025 this will entail extensive regrading of the creek channel, floodplain, and associated uplands; the removal of the remnants of the mill and its 20-plus acres of asphalt; habitat restoration; and the creation of a new trailhead and parking areas. Construction of the visitor center building and related site developments will also occur sometime in the future after its transfer to the National Park Service (NPS), but those improvements have yet to be scheduled by the NPS.

Existing Site: As we first encountered it, the site comprised a flat expanse of asphalt stripped of trees, blocked off from the Prairie Creek floodplain by a high earthen berm, and surrounded by the second-growth redwood forest that has grown up since the clear-cutting of the majority of the area's old-growth trees. The mill's buildings were long

The former mill had severed the surrounding uplands and forests from the riparian zone and wetlands, and in so doing, had created an industrial wasteland in place of the interconnected ecological system that nurtured the magnificent coastal redwood forests.

gone, but pieces of their former concrete foundations still popped up irregularly out of the disintegrating asphalt, complete with rusted bolts and protruding steel reinforcing bars. At the wet margins of the former lumber yard, aggressive roots from pioneering alder, willow, and cottonwood trees had begun to heave the paving. It was easy to imagine that the entire 20-acre field of asphalt could be reclaimed by the surrounding forest within a few decades.

In terms of wildlife, there was evidence of a recent visit by a herd of native Roosevelt elk. Osprey nests could be seen in the uppermost snags of the hillside forest. The telltale markings of black bear were also present in the form of bark stripped from young trees. A praying mantis had made a home in an open pipe, and marbled murrelets were nesting in the remaining old-growth trees. Interestingly, Prairie Creek itself, despite decades of degradation due to the development of this and neighboring sites, teemed with wild coho salmon. Clearly this was a place where nature might once again prevail. Our work would be to guide the process of its recovery while creating a mutually supportive new built environment.

Yurok Heritage: The site is part of the ancestral lands of the Yurok Tribe, a Native people who have lived in this area for thousands of years. Although the site is not part of their nearby reservation lands, the natural and cultural heritage of the Yurok, their approach to land stewardship, and their understanding that people are a part of nature informed the planning and design of all aspects of the Prairie Creek restoration and visitor center development. The Yurok Tribe together with the local non-Native community were engaged as full partners in conceptual planning, design, and stewardship of the site. And their involvement will continue throughout future work in the ecological restoration, development, and programming of activities.

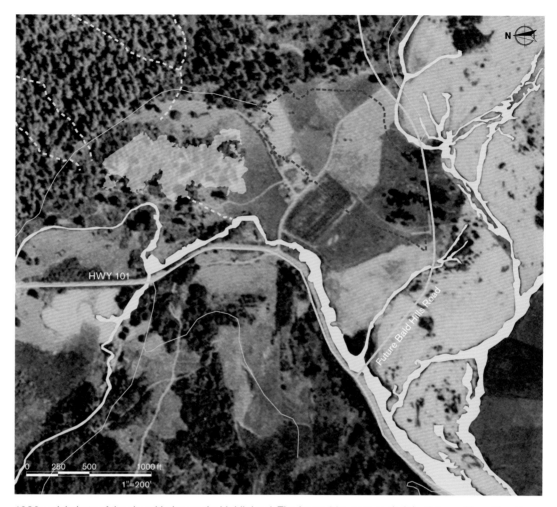

1936 aerial photo of the site with the creeks highlighted. The future 20+-acre asphalt lumber yard is outlined in red. 2015. JNRA.

Overall Site Design: The former mill had severed the surrounding uplands and forests from the riparian zone and wetlands, and in doing so had created an industrial wasteland in place of the former interconnected ecological system that had nurtured the area's magnificent coastal redwood forests. Decades of alterations to Prairie Creek, including the construction of roadways, bridges, culverts, and channel reconfigurations, had likewise led to an unnatural pattern of siltation, deepened the creek channel, and separated it from its natural floodplain. Addressing this pattern of degradation at both the old mill site and in the channel of Prairie Creek required that the overall site be treated as a single integrated redesign challenge. A regrading of the entire site, the recycling of ground-up asphalt, and the reuse of gravel fill to reshape nearby landforms would thus be key aspects of site engineering, ecological restoration, and the eventual visitor experience.

Prairie Creek floodplain with the lone-surviving Centennial Tree rising within a second-growth redwood forest.
2016. JNRA.

The existing 20+-acre asphalt-paved lumber yard will be removed, and the site regraded for the future visitor center to reconnect with the Prairie Creek floodplain. 2016. JNRA.

The primary work needed to restore the healthy ecological functioning of Prairie Creek involved reconnecting its deeply incised channel with its floodplain. Extensive excavation would be required to lower the floodplain and create habitat-rich backchannels and wetlands. Meanwhile, excavated floodplain soils and gravels could be used in combination with recycled asphalt to raise the future site of the visitor center complex above the 500-year flood line, and above a low-lying coastal zone potentially at hazard from tsunami inundation —primary considerations to ensure the safety of public-serving facilities in the face of projected sea-level rise. Regrading could also be used to knit the site together into a spatial and ecological continuum of restored habitats from the creek to the forested hillsides, with public access in the uplands separated from the most sensitive areas in the lowlands. Our first task was thus to work in close coordination with the restoration engineers and biologists to establish an overall site grading concept. They could then focus on the restoration of Prairie Creek while we focused on the design of the visitor center site.

Rendering of the future visitor center and the restored site of the former lumber yard integrated with restored natural landscape of Prairie Creek. 2022. JNRA, NHE. Rendering by Studio 5411.

Visitor Center: As the primary attraction for those coming to the site, the new visitor center will one day serve as a threshold for the experience of surrounding state- and federally protected redwood forests. As a point of arrival, its purpose will be to orient visitors to the larger landscape and influence all aspects of public access to it. All supporting site developments, such as parking, bus drop-off, outdoor gathering spaces, overlooks, trail connections, and interpretive facilities, will spin off from the location selected for the building. The building and related site developments will thus form the place from which activities are organized and at which visitors will be introduced to the ecological richness of the redwood region.

The proposed building design is shaped by its site. Located on high ground at the upper end of the former lumber yard and backed by the towering redwood forests on the surrounding hills, it will occupy a commanding position with panoramic vistas up and down the valley, across meadow landscapes, and toward the surrounding forests. Its form consists of two segments linked at the center at an open angle and rising dramatically at either end.

Proposed Visitor Center building. 2016. Siegel & Strain Architects.

One wing will be oriented to an old-growth redwood grove on the hillside above, the site of marbled murrelet and osprey nests; the other will be oriented to the restored creek, floodplain, and wetlands. The space between the wings meanwhile is conceived as a gateway through which visitors may either enter the realm of the hillside redwoods forests beyond or descend to the valley bottom to follow trails downstream to the ocean. By design the building is meant to serve as a spatial frame, capturing the varied landscapes that make this place, and it will be complemented by a series of outdoor plazas, gathering areas, and educational features intended to extend and complement it. Among these will be interpretive exhibits, quiet seating, an amphitheater, and gardens where visitors will be able to learn about and marvel at the surrounding multilayered native landscape.

As important as the building is, however, the combination of built and natural landscapes will be what gives identity to this place. Before reaching the visitor center complex, visitors will follow a path designed to reveal the whole spectrum of the site ecology. As this sequence unfolds, the first view from the access roadway and coastal trail will be of the restored creek and floodplain, framed by groves of redwoods, because it is water that links this place with all other places upstream and down. Then, as the roadway and trail curve away from the floodplain, visitors will be afforded a glimpse of the distant visitor center building across a restored elk meadow. From here the building will appear as a small structure against the backdrop of towering trees. The curving roadway will then straighten to align directly with a remnant old-growth redwood forest on the hillside — the iconic beings that thrive in this landscape. And, after one final curve in the road as it rises toward the end of the upland meadow, the building itself will be revealed at close range sitting dramatically on open ground at the edge of the forests, with parking tucked into restored woodlands to one side. The journey through the restored wildlands will thus serve as foreground to the preserved natural setting, and it will tell the story of the rehabilitation of this place, its heritage, and its rebirth.

Trails Gateway: The first phase of construction includes the removal of asphalt and the regrading of more than 200,000 cubic yards of dirt and gravel to reintegrate the upland site with the Prairie Creek floodplain. The resultant new landforms will then be revegetated, and wildlife habitats restored. A trailhead with parking, trail connections, restrooms, and seating made from trees removed during the construction will be created. The proper conditions will also be established for the construction of the future visitor center building, its parking areas, and related site improvements by the National Park Service. In the meantime, the fully accessible site will be treated as an ecological recovery zone knitted into the fabric of the surrounding forests and streams — a living tribute to the vision of those who have worked for many years to restore and protect this remarkable place.

The extent of the earth-moving in this project is unusual, due largely to the past degradation of the site. The ground plane is the fundamental building block of both the natural landscape and the built environment. When conceived together, a harmonious balance can be achieved. Careful grading to direct the flow of water, the life force of nature, establishes the ecological framework for the integrated development and knits the whole site together. In this case, the sculpted landform was conceived to blend with the natural contours of the site as it existed before the mill, while establishing a foundation for planned future construction. The land was reshaped by rerouting creek channels, excavating for wetlands, lowering elevations of flood overflow fields, and carving out backflow channels while filling the upland areas for public access, flood protection, forest expansion, and views of the landscape.

Once the phase 1 trails gateway site improvements are completed, a portion of the site to the north of the future building between a tributary stream and the floodplain wetlands will also be dedicated to the Yurok Tribe as a ceremonial site. In addition, the proximity of the trails gateway to the town of Orick will bring much needed economic activity to this local community. This thoughtfully conceived built environment will thus offer visitors a rich natural wildland experience while supporting surrounding communities — a new balance as meaningful as the health of the natural systems that will be restored. ⊛

Right page: The site will be regraded to create high ground for the Trails Gateway and future Visitor Center while integrating the uplands with the floodplain. 2021. JNRA.

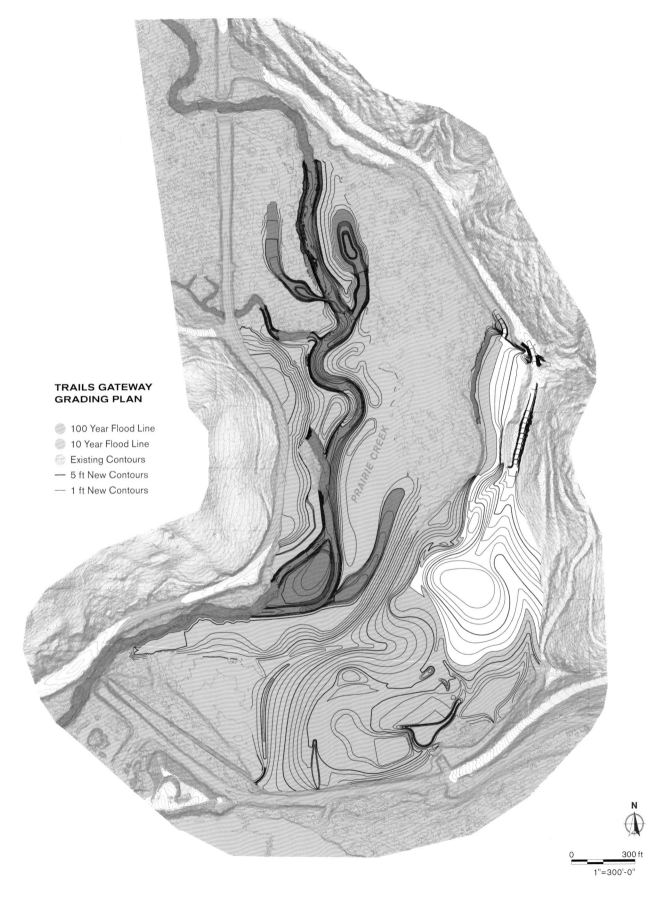

**TRAILS GATEWAY
GRADING PLAN**

100 Year Flood Line
10 Year Flood Line
Existing Contours
— 5 ft New Contours
— 1 ft New Contours

PRAIRIE CREEK

N

0   300 ft
1"=300'-0"

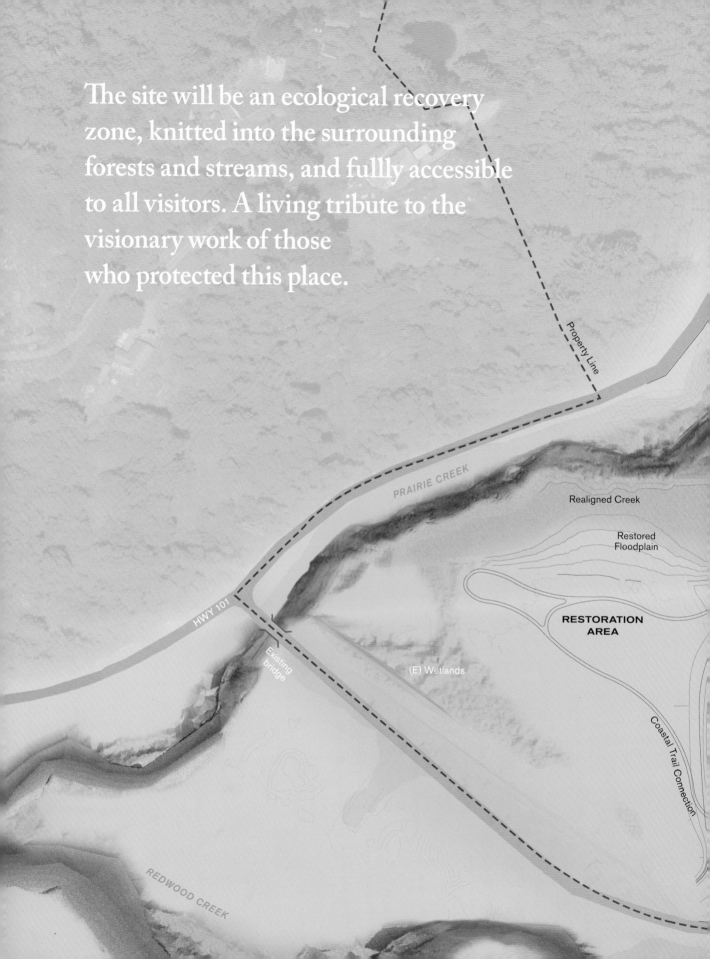

The site will be an ecological recovery zone, knitted into the surrounding forests and streams, and fullly accessible to all visitors. A living tribute to the visionary work of those who protected this place.

Property Line

PRAIRIE CREEK

Realigned Creek

Restored Floodplain

HWY 101

RESTORATION AREA

Existing bridge

(E) Wetlands

Coastal Trail Connection

REDWOOD CREEK

(E) Wetlands

Realigned Creek

Backwater Channel

Restored Riparian Forest

Restored Floodplain

Yurok Village Site

Upper Trail - Emergency Evacuation Trail

Walk the length of a Redwood Exhibit

Amphiteather

Bike Parking

VISITOR CENTER

Outdoor Classroom

Coastal Trail

10 Year Flood Line

100 Year Flood Line

Shuttle, Bus Stop & Drop Off

Parking

Old Growth Redwood Forest

RV & Bus Parking

Restored Forest

Property Line

100 Year Flood Line

Leach Field Area

Utility Yard

Entry Parking

Redwood Creek Trail Connection

Kiosk

Bald Hills RD

Security Gate & Fence

10 Year Flood Line

N

0   50   100   200   300   400 ft

1"=100'

CODA

The transformations of the places described in this book occurred during a period of radical social and environmental change. Taken together and individually, these stories reflect ways in which a fragile, complex shift in our Eurocentric culture has manifested itself in places that make up our common landscape. They provide a window into a new ecological and social ethic that has been emerging over the past half century, marking the beginning of a redefinition of our human relationships with nature and with each other. Empowered community voices guiding the conception of the public commons are making our spaces inclusive, equitable, and responsive to our cultural diversity. These are stories about changes to small and large public spaces where healthy ecological systems and community bonds have created the setting for everyday life. Step by step, incremental improvements such as these that touch people personally can gradually build to effect broader changes and redefine the basis for future choices.

Despite this progress (or perhaps because of it), renewed pressure for deeper change has grown in recent years, brought about in large part by unresolved mistakes from the past, cultural intransigence, and limitations in the historic "human-dominant" frame of reference. The strength of our emerging environmental and cultural ethic is being

Left page: A trail along the ecologically rich river corridor commons created through community activism in the heart of Petaluma linking neighborhoods with downtown. 2021. Jose Luis Aranda.

challenged. The potentially catastrophic consequences of global warming, sea-level rise, a resource-extraction-based economy, income disparities, and systemic racism seem to dwarf the issues that were at the forefront decades ago. These emerging concerns are, indeed, enormously complex, and urgently demand new approaches. But so have been many of the issues successfully confronted in the past. Real systemic cultural change has just begun, and a powerful base has been created on which to build a more resilient, equitable future.

As the consequences of our past failed attempts at domination have been revealed, we are beginning to see that we must learn to live with nature. One critical lesson is that ecological sustainability and community health must go hand in hand if we are to confront seemingly intractable issues. Stewardship for future generations will require an even deeper cultural shift to honor unconditionally and equitably all those who inhabit the commons, to repair the disconnect between humans and nature, and to value the interdependence of all life. These and other stories of change to our commons demonstrate that the built and natural environments can coexist harmoniously. We are part of, not separated from, the "wildlands." Even better, as institutions and as individuals we must understand that the meaning of the term itself will change. "Wilderness" can no longer be seen as something apart from "civilization," to be conquered for us to survive; it must be seen as something essential to be embraced for our survival.

Technologies will inevitably change, and technological advances will be essential for correcting past mistakes and avoiding others in the future. But resolutions to our present dilemmas will not be simply technological. They will be a blend of ancient ecological and cultural wisdom with modern science and technology. Underlying the continuing and necessary cultural shift that will sustain the next generations must be the deep commitment to protect the earth, to nurture natural systems, to live with nature, and to maintain equity among all living things.

These are community-wide challenges, demanding focused collaborative attention by individuals, neighborhoods, private interests, philanthropic enterprises, and our public institutions alike. All will and must have a voice in the design of new and transformed places that will support our common needs while nurturing and sustaining life on this planet. Those who take on the physical design challenges must listen, observe, absorb information, and respond with new insight.

Common to all these stories about placemaking are communities of people who have engaged in creative processes to transform the physical environment. Some were grassroots efforts inspired by individuals or groups who initiated the changes themselves in response to past transgressions, new opportunities, or changed circumstances. Others were efforts initiated by government or nonprofit agencies that manage resources for public benefit. Still others were efforts by private property owners who understood the benefits of healthy ecology and a vibrant public realm. In each case, the projects were driven by people committed to public well-being who joined together to create a better place. And in each case, ordinary people had a voice in envisioning the new physical environment reflecting rediscovered ecological wisdom and supportive community life. Those voices that influenced the design of the places were expressing a faith in the future based on a belief that their efforts would make a difference for the people themselves and for coming generations. The same is true today and will be so tomorrow.

Places that people inhabit don't simply assemble themselves. Someone needs to draw the line on a plan to give scale to each individual space, to integrate the various pieces into a whole, and to compose a balance between the built and natural environments. The designer is critical to the work as both collaborator and guide, offering creative, practical, technical, and humane expertise. A designer of the physical environment is thinking about the qualities of spatial volumes, the experience of being within or moving through space, the technologies and systems that support the space, the practicalities of building and maintaining the place, the uses for the space, the environmental implications of the choices made, the insights of the users, the cultural context, the regulatory framework, and a myriad of other factors. Community input, scientific data, and cultural values are essential ingredients for spatial design. They form the foundation for the creation of places, frame the program of uses to be accommodated, establish the goals for a project, and clarify the criteria for success or failure.

As important as the designer is in bringing all the information together into a coherent, beautiful, and responsive physical environment, humility is an important ingredient in ecologically based community design. The designer is a guide, educator, listener, and creative force. But everyone who participates in the design process plays an important role in the creation of the place, including the people, animals, trees, water, stone, and soil of the place itself. The place that is made will reflect the contributions of each. Once the construction is over, the place will belong to the people and critters who use it. It is important that the place work for them. Those who will be responsible for the place and live with it must believe in what has been created. They are the ones who will look after it long after the project is done.

Our human and ecological relationships have changed dramatically over the past half century as we have confronted past mistakes and reset our priorities. The emerging cultural shift is reflected in the increasing ecological wisdom underlying the transformation of our public commons and an increasing embrace of diversity. Our culture has the potential to become even more ecologically and socially responsible if we continue to open ourselves to new possibilities. As nature increasingly asserts its authority, our very survival will depend upon it. We have no other choice at this stage but to adapt together with creativity, insight, and wisdom. But how we adapt is up to us. Without deep, fundamental cultural changes we face the likelihood of falling back on old patterns and thwarting the opportunity to design places, large and small, that are socially equitable, ecologically diverse, and sustainable over time. ⊛

Following page: Passing through a preserved oak woodland in the Orinda hills. 2016. Hanh Nguyen.

ACKNOWLEDGMENTS

My wife, Jody, first encouraged me to write this book over a decade ago. She has been at my side and has supported my work from the beginning. She thought it was time for me to tell the stories. We have spent endless hours together in creative partnership talking through projects, wrestling with possibilities, visiting places, and enjoying the fruits of this work. Jody was a most helpful critic of the early drafts, and her editorial suggestions improved the stories significantly each step of the way. When I was finally ready to start the book, my Associate, Daniela P. Corvillon, enthusiastically stepped forward, diving in with insight and creativity. It turns out this was something she was very interested in doing as well. Together, we selected the stories to tell and discussed the central messages of each. She then organized the supporting photos, diagrams, maps, and other graphics, guiding the design and character of the book. I could not have done this without her.

It was Daniela who suggested that I hire Camila Undurraga as a graphic designer to help visualize what the book design might become. Camila was able to take the text, photos, graphics, and general layout that we sent to her and compose a beautiful, accessible document. Whatever hesitation I might have had about working remotely on a creative project with someone as far away as Patagonia was quickly assuaged when we looked at the first drafts together. Working with her has been a most rewarding collaboration. She is a marvel.

My twin brother, Bill Roberts, read through the early texts in detail and offered fundamental strategic suggestions as well as specific editorial improvements on individual stories. He graciously reviewed subsequent versions and has been a supporter each step of the way. As a general contractor who was trained as an architect, and who spends most of his spare time in parks and open spaces when he is not reading or writing, his insights have been extremely useful.

Others who reviewed early drafts and offered constructive encouraging comments include my son, David, my daughter, Taya, Dan Bedford, Jennifer Roberts, Erica Roberts, Kyra Baldwin, Pin Wang, Evany Zirul, Neal Roberts, my old college roommate Neil O'Donnell, David Hiller, Elizabeth Taylor, and Betsy Foster. My thanks to all of them.

At the point when I realized that this adventure might turn into a real book, I sought assistance from the editor of various professional journals who is also an architect colleague. David Moffat had edited two articles of mine in years past for the journal Places, and I thought he might be interested in this project. I was a little nervous but happy when he said he would look at what I had been doing and elated when he agreed to take on the editorial work. His keen insights into the work, deep knowledge of the field, and understanding of the professional literature have been more than what I had hoped for.

The projects in this book, and the stories themselves, are collaborations among many creative people, not just me alone. I would like to acknowledge those key collaborators with whom I have worked to make these stories come to life.

JOHN NORTHMORE ROBERTS & ASSOCIATES , INC. (JNRA) STAFF

My small Landscape Architecture office, John Northmore Roberts & Associates, Inc., has had a dedicated and talented staff that has slowly changed over the years. I asked them to apply their creativity in all phases of projects, and they pitched in enthusiastically to assist each other as needed. The people who participated in important ways in the projects of this book and preparation of the book graphics include, in alphabetical order: Kyra Baldwin, Maki Boyle, Margo Cantwell, Daniela P. Corvillon, Tanya Eggers, Dan Bedford, Ray Freeman, Alex Gunst, Lisa Howard, Ellie Insley, Tomi Kobara, Deena Ku, Michael Ludwig, Lorenzo Reynoso, Derek K. Schubert, and Rebecca Sunter and Pin Wang.

PHOTOGRAPHY

PHOTOGRAPHERS	José Luis Aranda Nucamendi, M.Sc., www.joseluisaranda.com
	Hanh Nguyen, Hanh Nguyen Photography, www.hanh-photos.com
	Ashley James, www.searchlightfilms.org
	John Northmore Roberts & Associates (JNRA) — John N. Roberts, Daniela Peña Corvillon
	National Park Service (NPS)
	Taya L. Roberts
	Elena Vasquez Valls
PHOTOGRAPHY EDITOR	Daniel Corvillon Achondo, www.danielcorvillon.com
AERIAL PHOTOGRAPHY PILOT	Daniel R. Bedford

GRAPHIC DESIGN

BOOK DESIGN	Camila Undurraga Puelma, www.camilaundurraga.art
INFOGRAPHICS	JNRA and Camila Undurraga Puelma

PROJECT DESIGN TEAMS

FORT MASON AND FORT MASON COMMUNITY GARDENS
Royston, Hanamoto, Beck, & Abey, Landscape Architects, John N. Roberts Associate
Golden Gate National Recreation Area

CRISSY FIELD
JNRA, Landscape Architects
Katsuo Saito, Landscape Architect
Philip Williams & Associates, Ltd., Hydrologists
Alan Gussow, Artist
Golden Gate National Recreation Area
Golden Gate National Parks Conservancy
Golden Gate National Recreation Area

EL POLIN SPRING
JNRA, Landscape Architects
Enginious Structures, Structural Engineers
Barth Campbell, Trails
Presidio Trust

PRESIDIO OFFICER'S CLUB
Perkins+Will, Architects
JNRA, Landscape Architects
Sherwood Design Engineers, Civil Engineers
Presidio Trust

BOEDDEKER PARK
WRNS Studio, Architects
JNRA, Landscape Architects
Sherwood Design Engineers, Civil Engineers
City of San Francisco, Recreation and Parks
City of San Francisco Arts Commission
Trust for Public Land

LIBRARY TERRACE GARDEN
JNRA, Landscape Architects
Edwin Hamilton, Artist
Strybing Arboretum

LOWER REDWOOD CREEK RESTORATION AND PUBLIC ACCESS
Philip Williams & Associates, Ltd., Hydrologists
JNRA, Landscape Architects
Stillwater Sciences, Restoration Biologists

Point Reyes Observatory, Biologists
OTAK, Landscape Architects and Engineers
Northern Hydrology & Engineering, Restoration Hydrologists
Enginious Structures, Bridge Structural Engineers
Golden Gate National Recreation Area
Golden Gate National Parks Conservancy

MUIR WOODS NATIONAL
MONUMENT

JNRA, Landscape Architects
Jerry Langkammerer, Architect
Golden Gate National Recreation Area
Golden Gate National Parks Conservancy

POCO WAY
NEIGHBORHOOD
REVITALIZATION

Herman Stoller Coliver, Architects
JNRA, Landscape Architects
San Jose Housing Authority
City of San Jose

MERCY BUSH
NEIGHBORHOOD PARK

JNRA, Landscape Architects
M. Alexander Gunst, Landscape Architect
Bak Zuhdi, Civil Engineer
City of Mountain View

COLMA HISTORICAL PARK
AND COMMUNITY CENTER

Page & Turnbull, Architects
JNRA, Landscape Architects
City of Colma

PETALUMA RIVER ACCESS
AND ENHANCEMENT PLA

JNRA, Landscape Architects
Wagstaff & Associates, Urban and Environmental Planners
Questa Engineering, Inc., Hydrologists and Biologists
Williams Kuebelbeck & Associates, Inc., Economists
Page & Turnbull, Inc., Architects
MIG, Community Participation
Citizens Advisory Committee (19 members)
Technical Advisory Committee (24 members)
City of Petaluma Planning Department
State Coastal Conservancy

CHARLES M. SCHULZ   C. David Robinson, Architects
MUSEUM AND RESEARCH   JNRA, Landscape Architects
CENTER   Lea Goode-Harris, Labyrinth Designer
                         Edwin Hamilton, Artist
                         Jeannie Schulz
                         Charles M. Schulz Museum

YOUNTVILLE TOWN   Susi Marzuola, Architect
CENTER   JNRA, Landscape Architects
                         Siegel & Strain, Architects
                         Coastland Civil Engineering
                         Citizen Advisory Committee (9 members)
                         Town of Yountville

STAG'S LEAP WINE   Javier Barba, Architect
CELLARS   JNRA, Landscape Architects
                         Stag's Leap Wine Cellars

ADDISON STREET ARTS   JNRA, Landscape Architects
DISTRICT   ELS, Architects
                         Susie Medak, Berkeley Repertory Theater
                         Robert L. Hass and Jessica Fisher, Poetry Walk
                         Scott Donohue, Artist
                         City of Berkeley Arts Commission
                         City of Berkeley Office of Economic Development

BERKELEY CENTRAL   Ripley/Boora Architects
LIBRARY AND LIBRARY   Thomas P. Cox, Architects
GARDENS/K STREET   JNRA, Landscape Architects
FLATS   Susan Pascal Beran, Jeff Reed, Jennifer Madden, Artists
                         John H. DeClercq, Library Gardens, L.P.

FOURTH STREET PASEO   Abrams & Milliken, Architects
                         Kahn Design Associates, Architects
                         JNRA, Landscape Architects
                         Hohbach-Lewin, Inc., Civil Engineers
                         Jamestown L.P.

NORTH WATERFRONT
PARK AND CESAR
CHAVEZ MEMORIAL
SOLAR CALENDAR

JNRA, Landscape Architects
Richard Haag Associates, Landscape Architects
Brooks Rand, Ltd., Chemical Engineers
MIG, Community Participation
Willard Bascom, Oceanography & Coastal Processes
University of California, Irvine, Department of Chemistry, F.S.
Rowland, Ph.D., and Donald Blake, Ph.D.
Citizens Task Force — Waterfront, Parks, Civic Arts, Solid Waste
Commissions — (20 members)
Santiago Casal, Solar Calendar Memorial
City of Berkeley Public Works Department
City of Berkeley Parks, Marina, and Forestry Division

YOSEMITE VILLAGE DAY
USE AREA

Jacobs Engineering, Roadway Engineers
JNRA, Landscape Architects
Seigel & Strain, Architects
Provost & Pritchard, Civil Engineers
Leslie Stone Associates, Wayfinding and Exhibits
Yosemite National Park Project Management

YOSEMITE LODGE AT THE
FALLS

Seigel & Strain, Architects
JNRA, Landscape Architects
Nelson Nygaard, Traffic Engineers
AECOM, Value Analysis
Jacobs Engineering, Roadway Engineers
Leslie Stone Associates, Wayfinding and Signage
Delaware North Corporation, Concessionaire
Aramark Corporation, Concessionaire
Yosemite National Park Project Management

BRIDALVEIL FALL ACCESS
AND REHABILITATION

JNRA, Landscape Architects
Seigel & Strain, Architect
Provost & Pritchard, Civil Engineers
EndreStudio, Structural Engineers
Leslie Stone Associates, Wayfinding and Signage
Yosemite National Park Project Management
Yosemite Conservancy

REDWOOD NATIONAL
AND STATE PARKS
VISITOR CENTER

Seigel & Strain, Architects
JNRA, Landscape Architects
Aldrich Pears Associates, Ltd., Interpretation and Exhibits
Sherwood Design Engineers, Civil Engineers
SHN Engineering Services, Civil and Geotechnical Engineers
Northern Hydrology & Engineering, Hydrology
McBain Associates, Restoration Revegetation
Redwood National Park
Prairie Creek Redwoods State Park
Cal Trout
Yurok Tribe
Save the Redwoods League

ONE

divides   fo. ever.

apparently twinned   identically gened

growing and changing   floating and tumbling,

sharing the prelude   entwining the other.

hearing before words   touching before hands.

Born whole.   Born apart.

Searching for   each missing

HA   LF

—John Roberts

ABOUT THE AUTHOR

John N. Roberts is the founding principal of the landscape architecture firm
John Northmore Roberts & Associates, Inc., located in Berkeley, CA. Since
1984, his firm has been committed to ecologically rooted, socially conscious,
and holistic site planning and design. His diverse, community-based practice has
focused on nearby places, with completed work throughout Northern California.
Mr. Roberts is a Beatrix Farrand Visiting Scholar at the University of California,
Berkeley, Department of Landscape Architecture and Environmental Planning
(LAEP), where he has taught as a Visiting Professor since 1984. He has taught
introductory design studios, technical design courses, and graduate design
studios, including Ecological Factors in Urban Landscape Design. He is a former
dancer and a published poet. His poem "One" is included in the Berkeley Poetry
Walk in downtown Berkeley's Addison Street Arts District. He and his wife of
53-years, Jody, have two children and four grandchildren.

By following the water and observing carefully we can discover stories of the place hidden in full view within both its large and intimate landscape setting, enjoyed by all the beings who share the space.